#noprojects
A Culture of Continuous Value

Evan Leybourn Shane Hastie

#noprojects: A Culture of Continuous Value

© 2018 Evan Leybourn, Shane Hastie. All rights reserved.

Published by C4Media, publisher of InfoQ.com.

ISBN: 978-1-387-94193-3

No part of this publication may be reproduced, stored in a retrieval system or transmitted in any form or by any means, electronic, mechanical, photocopying, recoding, scanning or otherwise except as permitted under Sections 107 or 108 of the 1976 United States Copyright Act, without the prior written permission of the Publisher.

Production Editor: Ana Ciobotaru
Copy Editor: Lawrence Nyveen
Design: Dragos Balasoiu

Contents

Introduction 13

The origin of projects 19

Where we went wrong 35

Outcomes over outputs 47

Value over busy 67

Adaptive portfolios 93

Delivering work 109

Continuous culture 121

Value-delivery teams 135

Funding #noprojects 155

#noprojects and business agility 177

Shane:

To Nancy - you've supported, inspired, put up with me and been a constant companion for the last 38 years. Thanks for everything - I love you!

Evan:

To Nilmini - thank you for being my biggest champion and driving me to create something amazing - I love you. Although, I would like to point out that you still haven't read my first book :)

Special Thanks:

To the fantastic team at InfoQ who did such a great job with editing, publishing and promoting this book - the professionalism, care and support made the "last mile" so much easier. Thanks!

About the authors

Evan Leybourn

Evan is the founder and CEO of the Business Agility Institute: an international membership body to both champion and support the next generation of organisations. These companies are agile, innovative, and dynamic — perfectly designed to thrive in today's unpredictable markets. His experience while holding senior leadership and board positions in both private industry and government has driven his work in business agility, and he regularly speaks on these topics at local and international industry conferences.

Evan is also the author of *Directing the Agile Organisation,* published by ITGP in 2013, and is a founding contributor to the Business Agility Library. But the greatest pride in his life is the time he spends raising an inquisitive and cunning little girl.

Shane Hastie

Shane Hastie is the director of agile learning programs for ICAgile (www.icagile.com), a global accreditation and certification body dedicated to improving the state of agile learning.

Since first using XP in 2000, Shane's been passionate about helping organisations and teams adopt sustainable, humanistic ways of working — irrespective of the brand or label they go by.

He was one of the core team who wrote version 3 of the Business Analysis Body of Knowledge (BABOK™) for the International Institute of Business Analysis (IIBA™) and led the joint Agile Alliance/IIBA™ team who wrote the Agile Extension to the BABOK™.

Shane was a director of the Agile Alliance (www.agilealliance.org) from 2011 until 2016. He is currently the chair of the Agile Alliance New Zealand, an affiliate organisation of the Agile Alliance.

Shane leads the Culture and Methods editorial team for InfoQ.com where he hosts the InfoQ Culture Podcast.

Case-study authors

Allan Kelly
Preface

Allan Kelly inspires, educates, and advises teams and executives creating digital products. He helps companies large and small enhance their agility and boost their digital offering. He has over 20 years software engineering experience and has spent the last 10 years advising companies and teams on agile and digital strategy.

He is the originator of value poker, time-value profiles, and retrospective dialogue sheets. Allan is the author of the perennial essay "Dear customer: The truth about IT projects" and books including *Xanpan: Team Centric Agile Software Development* and *Business Patterns for Software Developers*. His latest book is *Continuous Digital: An Agile Alternative to Projects for Digital Business*.

Doug Kirkpatrick
Haier elevation

Doug Kirkpatrick is an organisational-change consultant, TEDx and keynote speaker, blogger, educator, executive coach, dual citizen, and author of *Beyond Empowerment: The Age of the Self-Managed Organization*. He engages with Great Work Cultures, LeadWise, the Center for Innovative Cultures, and other communities to co-create the future of work. Doug enjoys travel in rough parts of the world and appreciates the perspective he gains from it.

Joanna L. Vahlsing
Evolving budget management

Joanna is a results-oriented-portfolio, program, project-management, and change leader with a 17+ year history of leading highly successful teams in enterprise-level and global environments. Her largest team numbered approximately 100 individuals and her largest managed budget topped $100 million. She is currently senior vice president of program management at Centro, an AdTech company headquartered in Chicago.

Joanna also enjoys giving back to the project-management and agile communities by volunteering her time as a mentor, serving as a content reviewer/SME for publications and international events, and presenting and hosting events.

Naresh Jain
Shipping is NOT success — let it sail!

Developer... consultant... conference producer... startup founder... struggling to stay up to date with technology innovation. Null-process evangelist Naresh Jain is an internationally recognized technology and product-development expert and the founder of ConfEngine. Over the last decade, he has helped streamline the product-development culture at many Fortune 500 companies like Google, Amazon.com, HP, Siemens Medical, GE Energy, Schlumberger, EMC, and CA Technologies. His hands-on approach to product innovation by focusing on product discovery and engineering excellence is a key differentiator.

Naresh founded the Agile Software Community of India and organises the Agile India conference. He is also responsible for organising 50+ international conferences including Functional Conf, Simple Design and Testing Conference, Agile Coach Camp, Selenium Conference India, Open Web & jQuery Conference, Open Data Science Conference India, and Eclipse Summit India. He has started many agile user groups including the Agile Philly User Group and groups in India. In recognition of his accomplishments, the Agile Alliance in 2007 awarded Naresh with the Gordon Pask Award for contributions to the agile community.

Larry Cooper
It's never just "an IT project"

Larry Cooper is a project executive and enterprise-transformation coach with 40+ years in the public and private sectors in Canada and the USA. He is a partner in AdaptiveOrg. Larry helps organisations of any size to transform complex and intransigent problems into simple, focused work that can be communicated and executed at all levels within an organization to achieve strategic intent.

Larry works with leaders and their teams to identify collaborative goals and the gaps in current strategic approaches. Together, they discover the portfolio, programs, and initiatives masquerading as large, overly complex, financially risky projects, so they know where to start to implement in the small while maintaining a steady focus on their short, medium, and long-term strategic priorities.

He is also an author, speaker, and webinar host who has hosted over 1,500 people in a single webinar.

Max Roy
Using the #noprojects paradigm

Max Roy is a driven IT professional who wants to make a difference in businesses. He is motivated to deliver projects that provide business intelligence in executive decision making.

Max's career has spanned over 25 years in roles such as solution/data architect, project manager, and IT faculty/trainer. Max has an innovative, pragmatic approach to addressing business needs and end-to-end delivery focus.

Max obtained a master's degree in IT from The Ohio State University and an MBA from the University of Maryland.

Preface by Allan Kelly

"Software is eating the world."

What more can Evan, Shane, or I say that Marc Andreessen hasn't?

Except now, five years on, the implications of a world run by software are becoming clearer. One of those implications is that the project model is not a suitable model for managing software development.

Just look at the car industry.

Look at Tesla.

Look how Google and Apple are making the news in the car industry — companies whose principal capability is creating software, not metal machines.

GM, Ford, Volkswagen, and company are scrambling to catch up, because right now the future is about technology capability and that technology is manifested as software.

While the car industry is playing out its digital transition in the public eye, countless companies and entire industries are wrestling with the same transition. In the process, opportunities arise for new entrants, disruptors, entrepreneurs, and intrapreneurs.

But the project model, with its demand to know the end of the digital story (and how much it costs) before the first chapter is even written, closes options and reduces value.

The defining feature of a project is that it is temporary, but software is permanent. The world that software teams are creating every day is not going away. Using a model based on the temporary to create the permanent creates confusion.

The project model offers a misplaced certainty. The project model says, "In this uncertain world, we can plan, we can identify the uncertainties, manage the risks, and deliver the thing you wanted."

How many project managers woke up on the morning of September 15, 2008 and found their plans in disarray? Was there a banking project in the world that didn't notice Lehman Brothers was gone? And how many of those RAID logs listed "Failure of a major financial institution"?

How many well-planned projects across Europe found on the morning of June 24, 2016 that they were no longer well planned? The uncertainty injected into not just the British but the entire European economy by the Brexit vote to leave the European Union will be here for years to come.

Similarly, how many projects in North America found on November 8, 2016 that plans and assumptions changed? Even though they had had two years to list "President Trump" in their RAID logs?

Melvyn King, former governor of the Bank of England, has suggested today's age is characterised by radical uncertainty: "uncertainty so profound that it is impossible to represent the future in terms of a knowable and exhaustive list of outcomes."

Some in the project community might offer projects and project planning as a means of tackling such uncertainty. But one must then ask at what cost?

Project planning and project management are not benign, free activities. Planning costs and project-management costs both add delay, and delay adds more costs. Insidiously, the project model itself undermines the quality of the thing it aims to deliver. And reducing quality adds costs, creates delays, and compromises the longevity of solutions.

The more risks, uncertainties, and contingencies the plans need to address, the greater the cost. The more comprehensive the plan, the bigger the plan, and the bigger the plan, the more it costs, and the higher the cost, the greater the belief in the plan, and the greater the belief, the harder it is to recognise problems. Big plans make for big cycles and slow change.

The process devalues and disempowers workers: why should a programmer bother to think when project preparation and managers have already done all the thinking needed?

Evan and Shane explore these problems and set out an alternative based on the same logic as agile: do something, see what happens, learn, then decide what to do next. Call it "inspect and adapt", call it "plan/do/check/act", call it the "Deming cycle" or "Shewhart cycle", call it "probing", call it "experimentation", call it "lean startup" — call it anything you like but keep doing it in tight loops.

As Evan and Shane describe here, #noprojects is capability based: capabilities to take action, to probe, to demonstrate value delivery, to learn, and to decide what action to take next. These aims may not sound that different than the aims of the project model but there is a world of difference in how the two models go about realising these aims.

Many, usually large, companies seem to have lost the ability to do; instead, they have the ability to plan. Watching them plan and then administer the plan into life reminds me of Frankenstein's efforts to force life into his monster.

The approach of planning and administration might have worked in 1970 when paper-based planning was far cheaper than CPU cycles, but today the reverse is true: CPU cycles are almost too cheap to meter. Companies that plan rather than code are vulnerable to disruption by those who, using cheap CPU cycles, do rather than plan.

The project model dates from the era of expensive CPU cycles. The Project Management Institute was founded in 1969 and Winston Royce first published his stepwise model (later called "waterfall") the following year.

IBM introduced the IBM System/360 Model 195 mainframe in 1970. The 195 provided 10 MIPS of processor power with 4 MB of RAM. It ran OS/360, used a hierarchical IMS database, and was programmed in languages such as COBOL and Fortran. Those lucky enough to have a real-time link to the machine used green-screen terminals or teletypes. (There were 13 internet nodes by the end of 1970.)

The Model 195 could cost $10 million although many firms preferred to rent for $250,000 per month — in 2016 dollars that is about $1.25 million per month.

In 2016, a Raspberry Pi 2 computer delivered 4,744 MIPS with 1 GB of RAM. It ran open-source Linux and could be programmed in Ruby, Scala, Python, Scratch, and many other advanced languages. You might choose to use a SQL database or a newly fashionable NoSQL hierarchical database. (There are currently over 5 billion Internet nodes and a couple of billion users.)

When introduced, the Pi sold for $35.

When CPU cycles were expensive, planning was cheap, and it made sense to outline as much as possible before touching the computer. Now that

CPU cycles are cheap, the planning needs of the project model make this approach hideously expensive.

Further, since 1970 our world has become massively more complex — not least because of the infrastructure of existing computer systems to deal with. And for good measure, add the complexity of globalisation, post-truth politics, and asymmetric warfare.

Given that the hardware, operating systems, databases, languages, and so much else of the technology landscape has changed, why would you expect a management model that dates from the 1960s to still apply today?

As every technologist should know, technology itself only delivers a small fraction of technology-enabled benefit; far more benefit is unleashed by subsequent process innovations that not only were not possible before the technology change but couldn't even be imagined.

Projects are not a God-given or natural phenomenon, they are a model of how to manage work. They are a human invention in the same way limited companies, capex, and social security are.

In this time of radical uncertainty and massive technological capability, isn't it time to consider how work is managed?

Ridding yourself of projects simplifies work and simplifies your thinking. #noprojects is the latest fellow traveller to join Douglas McGregor's Theory Y, agile software development, beyond budgeting, and emergent business strategy in mapping an alternative way of working.

For many, these ideas are too radical and represent too much risk. But for the few who embrace these ideas, they represent disruptive processes and competitive advantage over incumbent corporations.

You can write and change software without the project model — the two are not wedded. That does not mean one can ignore "building the right thing", ignore value delivery, or ignore risk management; neither can you ignore sustainable quality and cycle time, but for too long the project model has paid only lip service to the latter two.

#noprojects isn't the wild west and it isn't a licence to do what you whatever you like. By stripping away ceremonies and artefacts of the project model, #noprojects requires more discipline, more skill, and more involvement from team members.

In this book, Evan and Shane set out to challenge accepted thinking. Making sense of this requires readers to think for themselves. #noprojects is still young and still a work in progress. Evan and Shane cannot, and should not, answer every question; readers should instead start here to create their own answers.

— *Allan Kelly*

"If you don't see the value of the project construct in your organization, you're not alone. Shane and Evan have written a book explaining how you might create flow in your organization, to see and deliver the most valuable work faster.

— **Johanna Rothman**, Consultant and Author"

"At my company, Menlo Innovations, we have chosen a mission to 'end human suffering in the world as it relates to technology' and much of this suffering comes at the hands of very poorly run projects. Shane Hastie and Evan Leybourn, in their book #noprojects, give us a deep tour as to how we got here and a values-based roadmap on how to escape in order to bring joy back to technology, technology teams and the business that depend on them. There is a wealth of wisdom, expertise and experience shared that will give you a path to success that may be very different than the one you are now. Get ready for different and enjoy the ride!"

- **Richard Sheridan**
CEO, Chief Storyteller, Menlo Innovations
Author, Joy, Inc. - How We Built a Workplace People Love

"#noprojects is not about getting rid of projects and project managers, but about being able to continuously deliverer value to customers. It takes a culture where people work towards outcomes, a culture that truly embraces change and fosters continuous improvement as Evan and Shane explain in their book #noprojects - a culture of continuous value. The practices that support such a culture exist, let this book inspire you to apply them effectively to deliver more value to your customers."

- Ben Linders

#noprojects is a great read for people serious about putting products over projects. The authors blend new and novel ideas with tried and tested ideas from active, real world communities. As a reader, you will be respectfully challenged to throw out dogmatic, status quo ideas and replace them with tools and skills that foster learning from tangible and meaningful measurements. I've already recommended this book to a wide audience that includes program managers, big bosses, and product managers, and now I am doing the same to you.

- David Hussman

PART ONE

Introduction

#noprojects is a movement and a philosophy. It is not a "thing" and it is definitely not a methodology or a brand. It represents a set of principles, practices, and ideas that any organisation can apply. It doesn't have to be adopted as is; in fact, we want you to take these ideas, examine them for their applicability in your own context, use those which make sense in your environment, experiment with them, and adapt them as needed. We don't own the hashtag nor do we have any proprietary rights on the thinking behind the movement. We do care passionately about improving outcomes for organisations, teams, and individuals working in creative, knowledge-worker* environments.

This book is our response to the dismal failure rates that we see in projects, particularly in IT. Project thinking has caused problems in a VUCA[1] world where the rate of change exceeds most organisations' ability to respond to those changes, and the current project-based paradigm produces wasted effort, disastrous products, exhausted people,† and destroyed careers.

We want to be controversial for a moment and propose an end to projects and project management. We propose that the entire project process is flawed from the start for one simple reason: if you need to run a project, you've already failed.‡

By definition, a project is a "temporary endeavour undertaken to create a unique product, service, or result"[2] into an organisation. However, to be truly competitive, an organisation needs to be able to deliver a continuous stream of change. Managed properly, this negates the need for a project and the associated cost overheads.

The key word here is "**continuous**". While there may be fluctuations in demand and effort, there should be continuous, ongoing allocation of resources to maintain, enhance, and support most IT systems. If done properly, there should never be a need to run an "upgrade" project, a "version 2" project, a "maintenance" project, a "greenfield" project, or a "redevelopment" project. Even when creating something for the first time, a revolutionary change rather than an evolutionary change, a project struc-

---

* Most organisations are in the business of generating, recording, and using knowledge to create value in today's "information age". There are still some 20th-century industries where value is derived from leveraging muscles rather than brains, and for some of them the project paradigm still applies to at least a certain extent.

† And ruined marriages.

‡ As always, common sense applies. This is a dramatic and general statement and as such is generally true but not always specifically true.

ture explicitly defines an end: a point when the project or product will be done. Rather, it should be understood that every product is intended to achieve one or more business outcomes and, in order to do so, must continuously change and improve.*

This is fundamentally what #noprojects is. The approach, structure, tactics, and techniques available to successfully deliver continuous change. At its core, #noprojects is predicated on the alignment of activities to outcomes, measured by value, constrained by guiding principles, and supported by continuous-delivery technologies.[3]

There are always exceptions to #noprojects — work that is highly predictable and repeatable† or truly temporary.‡ A project structure can provide a clean break to allow these new ideas to flourish, but for most knowledge-worker organisations, this should be an exception and not the default delivery mechanism. Projects are exactly that, an exception to business as usual and you should be in the business of change.

You'll always come back to projects if you're building a literal bridge. You can't afford to change the plan once the concrete starts pouring. And once the bridge is built, you can't add new major features to it. It has already achieved the maximum potential value.§ While you need to maintain the value already created, there's not much left to create. This is in direct contrast to knowledge-worker industries where the creation and realisation of value is continuous, right up to the natural end of life. There is no longer a distinction between "build" and "maintain".

You still need to plan for the future — there is a lot of value in planning.¶ The intellectual rigours of identifying the desired outcomes and considering different ways to achieve them are important aspects of effective product development. Adaptive planning, an experimentation mindset, and ability to rapidly change direction are key elements for success in the 21st century — #noprojects is built on these ideas.

These ideas didn't spring into existence over the last couple of years** while we've been writing this book — many of them have been around for decades, and some for centuries. We draw on our own experiences in

---

* Until the natural end of its life, when it should be gracefully decommissioned.
† Such as a production line.
‡ Such as corporate mergers, construction projects, or (ironically) writing a book.
§ Even if that value is only realised over many years, every time a car drives over it.
¶ Although, honestly, not that much value in the plan itself.
** Waaaay longer than we intended when we first discussed putting our thoughts on paper.

implementing them, coaching and supporting others as they implemented them, and gleefully borrowing from the experience and wisdom of a community of practitioners and thought leaders in the space: people like Allan Kelly,[4] Joshua Arnold,[5] Steve Smith,[6] Rob England,[7] Pat Reed,[8] the 80-plus members of the #noprojects Slack community,[*] and many others.[†]

#noprojects frees us from the triple constraints of time, cost, and scope — the false deities of project management that mindlessly drive you towards a fixed deadline and an "all or nothing" result. The reality is that most of the requirements that go into the project plan (or backlog, if you're taking an agile approach) are at best wild-assed guesses about what some representative user might want, validated by a subject-matter expert, and are at least a year out of date. It is easy to claim success[‡] when only measuring by the triple constraint, but when measured against business outcomes, benefits delivered, customer satisfaction, and team engagement, results are dismal. All too often our organisational metrics don't include these factors.[§]

But don't fall into the trap of treating continuous change as one long project.[¶] There are some common activities that are needed in all #noprojects approaches:

- Start by defining the intended outcomes in terms of the metrics that actually matter, rather than the easy-to-measure vanity metrics.[9]
- Identify the first small step or experiment that will validate[**] the assumptions you are making towards achieving the outcomes.
- Execute that step.
- Measure the results.
- Inspect the process and adapt to the reality of what you've learned.
- Finally, repeat for the next step, pivot, or stop if you've either done enough, reached maximum value, or learned enough.

These ideas are founded on the deep respect for people as the primary source of innovation and value in organisations.

---

[*] And we encourage you to join the conversation here: https://noprojects.slack.com/
[†] If we missed mentioning you, we apologise — our influencers have been wide and varied and our memories shallow and narrow.
[‡] And get your bonus.
[§] Probably because they are embarrassing and hard to measure.
[¶] No matter how agile.
[**] Or disprove.

The most important question that #noprojects challenges you to ask is "What's it worth?" These three words are probably the most important words in the entire book. If you can't answer this question, you need to have a good look at the work that you are doing and evaluate why it's being done at all. If you can't even ask this question, you've got serious cultural problems inside your organisation and nothing we can say will overcome these problems for you.

Let us finish with the key principle behind this. Everything is a change; treat it accordingly. Change is done by, for, and to people. Treat them with respect and they will create value. This is #noprojects.

PART TWO

The origin of projects

When we started research for this book, we were surprised to discover that, while the abstract concept of a "project" is as old as humanity itself, the modern definition of a project and the associated domain of project management are surprisingly young — only a little over 60 years old. The history of projects is the Sisyphean effort to create predictability in an unpredictable environment with ever-increasing spending and ever-increasing risk.

Prior to the 1950s, countries, militaries, and companies didn't create projects as we understand them, but rather acts of nation-building, war, or engineering. These weren't led by project managers, but by engineers, architects, generals, and craftspeople.[1] While the history of project management isn't a straight line, it is generally accepted that it was during the 1950s that the convergence of practice, process, and management theory turned project management from a craft to a profession.

Today, we can define project management as "an advanced, specialised branch of management"[2] or more specifically, a project as "a temporary endeavour undertaken to create a unique product, service, or result".[3] Remember that definition — we'll come back to it shortly.

But let's go back a bit.

Daniel Defoe (of Robinson Crusoe **fame) wrote on the topic of projects** in 1697.[4] His series of essays is a truly fascinating read and provides great insights into how these grand projects[*] were funded. Defoe was highly critical of the "projectors" (what we would call investors) but recognised that many projects had left a positive legacy on the world.

> *Invention of arts, with engines and handicraft instruments for their improvement, requires a chronology as far back as the eldest son of Adam, and has to this day afforded some new discovery in every age....*
>
> *I shall trace the original of the projecting humour that now reigns no farther back than the year 1680, dating its birth as a monster then, though by times it had indeed something of life in the time of the late civil war. I allow, no age has been altogether without something of this nature, and some very happy projects are left to us as a taste of their success; as the water-houses for supplying of the city of London with water, and, since that, the New River — both very considerable undertakings, and perfect projects, adventured on the risk of success.*

---

[*] Be they nation building or war machines.

> *In the reign of King Charles I, infinite projects were set on foot for raising money without a Parliament: oppressing by monopolies and privy seals; but these are excluded our scheme as irregularities, for thus the French are as fruitful in projects as we; and these are rather stratagems than projects. After the Fire of London, the contrivance of an engine to quench fires was a project the author was said to get well by, and we have found to be very useful. But about the year 1680 began the art and mystery of projecting to creep into the world.*

Even many project management tools and visualisations trace their origins back centuries. The bar chart can be traced back to 1765 in Joseph Priestley's "Chart of Biography".[5]

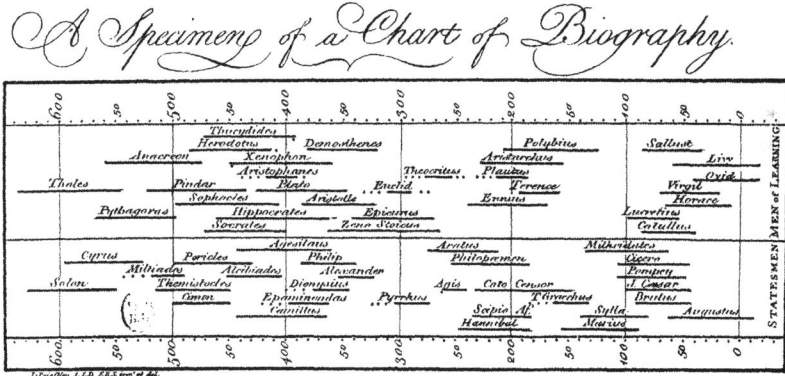

A redacted version of Priestley's "Chart of Biography" (1765).

Priestley designed this chart as part of his book *Lectures on History and General Policy*[6] so that students could "trace out distinctly the dependence of events to distribute them into such periods and divisions as shall lay the whole claim of past transactions in a just and orderly manner".*

Priestly subsequently inspired William Playfair to develop the bar chart as we know it today in his book from 1786, *The Commercial and Political Atlas*.[7] Playfair is also generally credited with inventing the line, area, and pie charts.

---

* That sounds a lot like a Gantt chart to us.

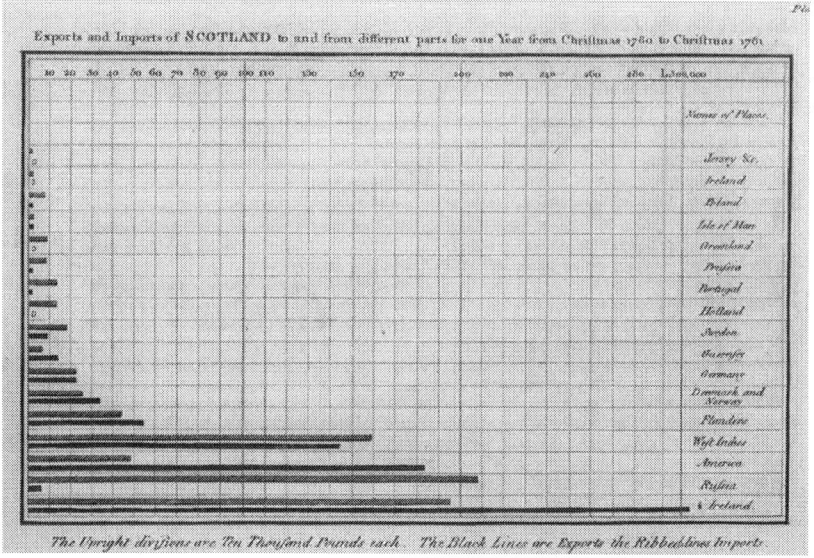

The first bar chart, from Playfair's The Commercial and Political Atlas (1786).

This all began to converge between the 1750s and 1850s as the Industrial Revolution completely transformed how people worked. Nowhere is this more evident than in our favourite quote from Adam Smith's *The Wealth of Nations*.[8] Smith drew a comparison from the craft of pin making and the role of the talented pin-maker who "...could not make 20 [pins in a day]. But in the way in which this business is now carried on..., I have seen a small manufactory where 10 men only were employed. Those 10 persons could make among them upwards of 48,000 pins in a day." And he was right — easily mechanised and repeatable tasks could produce goods faster and of higher quality* than anything that came before.

Everywhere you look, you can see the legacy of the Industrial Revolution, both positive and negative. This industrial mentality has shaped the way people work for centuries and continues to do so today. Modern project management's plan and work breakdown structure has more in common with the predictable segmentation of work in our pin-making factory than we give it credit for. Understanding this relationship is a key premise behind #noprojects and demonstrates some of the issues with project management as it is currently defined. Much of the work that you do today, especially knowledge work, is unique and innovative and has more in common with the talented pin-maker than with a pin-making factory. It is for this reason that, in our experience, creating accurate and useful

---

* Or at least more consistent quality.

work breakdown structures and project management plans is impossible in any meaningful way.

As industry and products became more complex, so did tools and visualisations. In 1896, Karol Adamiecki created the harmonogram, a floating-bar chart that showed tasks or resources over time. A little while later, Henry Gantt independently developed the Gantt chart* as a visualisation tool, which was used to help improve the manufacture of munitions and naval aircraft during World War I.[9] These charts were designed to compare expected production with actual output to allow easy identification of variance. The modern Gantt chart's pervasiveness is evidence of how drastically it affected how we measure and track production to this day.

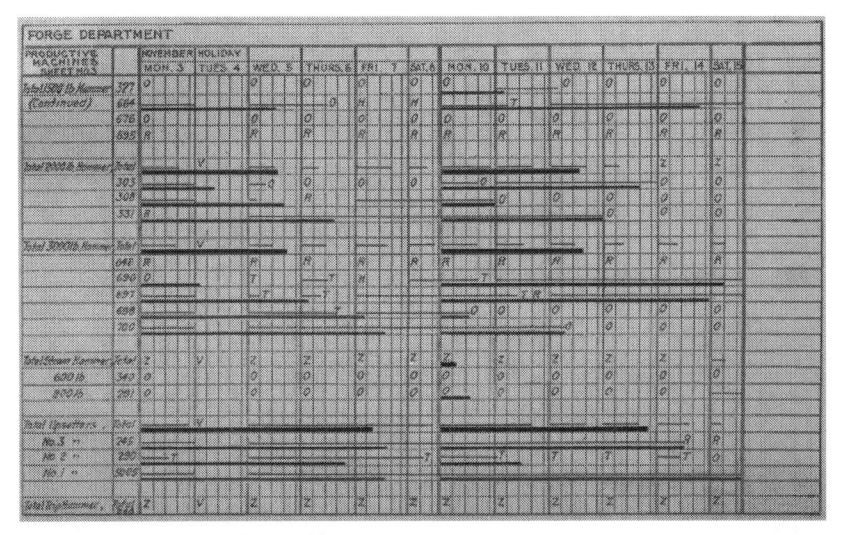

An early production Gantt Chart.

But it was only during the 1900s to 1950s that the origins of what we now call project management emerged.[10] Its immediate precursor would have to be Taylorism and scientific management. Published in 1911, Frederick Winslow Taylor's *Principles of Scientific Management*[11] outlined ways to increase worker productivity. Taylor studied labour-intensive and repetitive activities in detail — for example, loading iron from steel mills into a railcar — identifying where each individual action could be optimised to improve productivity and reduce error. Considered progressive for his time, Taylor even noted fatigue as an attribute to be analysed to improve productivity — in this case by recommending rest breaks to allow labourers to recover. Don't assume that this meant that Taylor was a champion

---

* Amongst others.

of workers' rights; he considered workers as resources to be used as efficiently as possible. Compared to previous ways of working, businesses saw scientific management as highly effective even though it required a higher manager-to-worker ratio and, by today's standards, would be considered micromanagement.

And that was one of the greatest criticisms of scientific management: the disenfranchisement of individual workers who were reduced to being highly focused "automen" without connection to the total production. This and other reductionist approaches worked well in simple domains but before long were replaced by system-wide approaches, although you can still see this reductionist model used in modern project management in the form of the work breakdown structure (WBS).

Even though scientific management is largely obsolete, we owe a debt to Taylor for introducing the scientific method and empiricism into management models. Taylor rejected the idea that trades were craft and believed that they could be studied, improved, and mechanised. Many of Taylor's observations on motivation and productivity continue to inform modern management — including #noprojects. In many ways, scientific management was the culmination of the Industrial Revolution's factory management model.

Project management started to emerge as a discrete concept in the 1920s and 1930s. The earliest formal usage we can find is from the US Bureau of Reclamations, which created a "project office" with a "project engineer" leading a project.[1] The role of "project coordinator" emerged at roughly the same time in the US aircraft industry.

Coming into the 1930s, massive construction endeavours began to use project management. In 1931, the Empire State Building was delivered ahead of time and under budget — attributed to the use of location-based scheduling (specifically flow-line scheduling). The effectiveness of flow-line scheduling and other types of location-based scheduling, such as the US Navy's line-of-balance (LOB) technique,[12] were indisputable, and so were used to schedule repetitive projects such as pipelines, high rises, and railway projects. We were a little surprised to learn that not all construction projects used these methods. For example, in 1936, the Hoover Dam was successfully completed under budget and ahead of schedule using the good old Gantt Chart.

No history of projects would be complete without at least mentioning the Manhattan Project (1942-1945), probably one of the most famous* projects of the era.

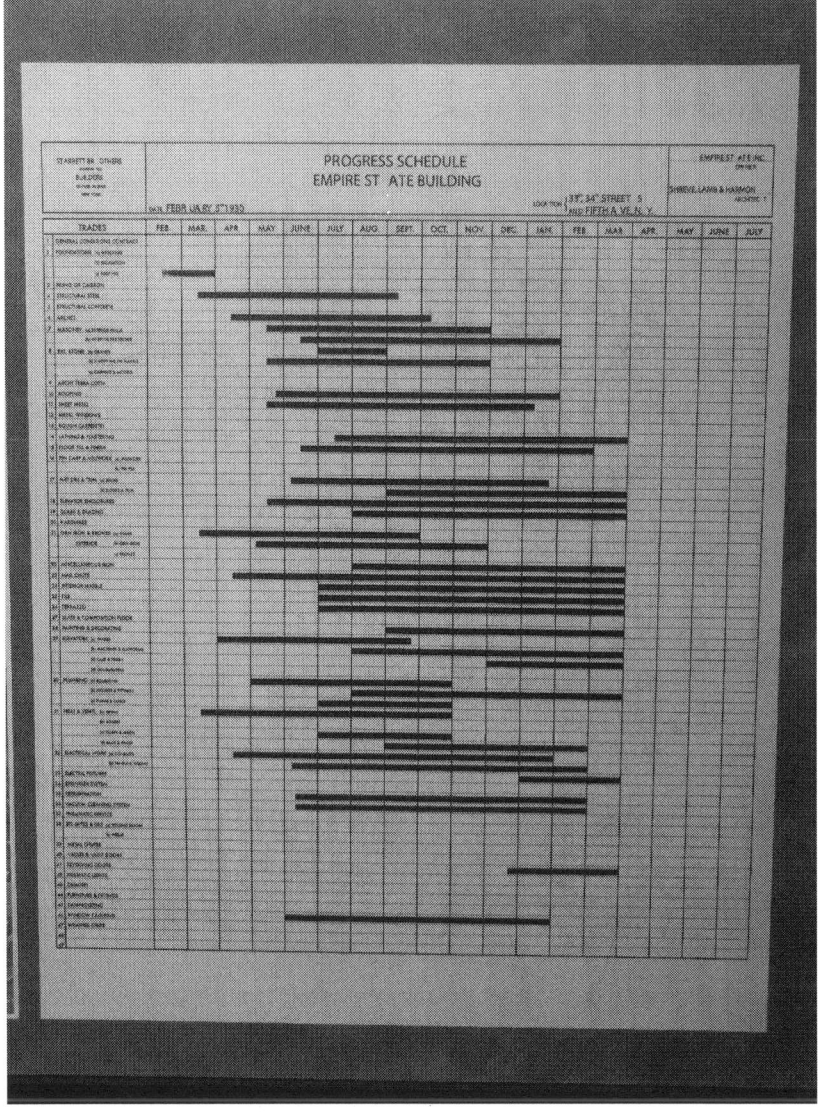

Progress schedule for the Empire State Building (1930).

As far as we can discover, the first use of the title "project manager" seems to have occurred around 1953 in the aerospace industry — specifically, in

---

* Or should that be "infamous"?

the Glenn L. Martin Company* and McDonnell Aircraft.[13] That said, these early roles didn't have many of the same responsibilities that you would attribute to a modern project manager.

The first project, in the modern sense of the word, would probably have occurred in DuPont in 1957. James Kelley of DuPont and Morgan Walker of Remington Rand10 developed a series of mathematical algorithms to track the relationships between individual activities, effort, and time that would later become the critical-path method (CPM). CPM[14] constructs a model of a project that defines all the required activities and the dependencies amongst them. Using an estimated duration of each activity, CPM calculates the longest path of sequential activities which together meet the project goal and the earliest and latest that any activity can start and finish without extending the project.

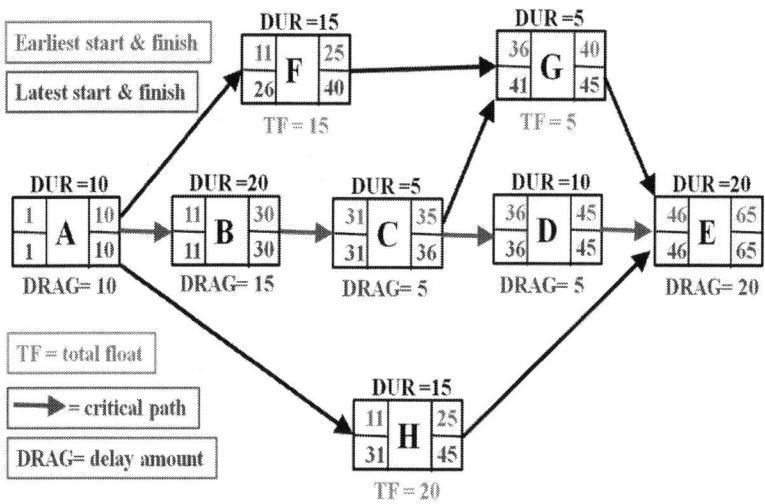

Activity-on-node diagram showing critical-path schedule, along with total float and critical-path drag computations.[15]

At about the same time, Booz Allen Hamilton and the US Navy developed the program evaluation and review technique (PERT)[16] for the Polaris submarine program. Conceptually similar to CPM, PERT is a statistical tool for analysing and representing the tasks involved in a project and determining the minimum time needed to complete the total project. These

---
* Which would become Lockheed Martin after a series of mergers.

methods allowed the creation of projects on a scale never seen before. The most impressive adoption would have to be NASA using PERT to maintain and schedule the Apollo missions, including the six successful moon landings.

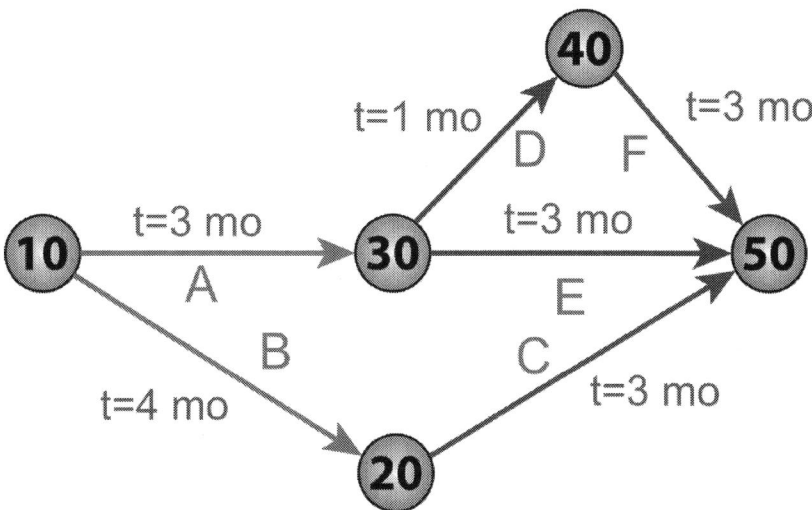

PERT network chart for a seven-month project with five milestones (10 through 50) and six activities (A through F).[17]

It would be remiss of us not to mention programme management[*] at this point. As a model of encapsulating multiple initiatives,[†] formal programme management probably predates formal project management. Going back to our NASA example, Apollo was actually a programme of work managed through the Apollo programme office. As well as managing each of the projects, the Apollo programme office was also responsible for managing procurement, contracts, and overall performance.

Beyond CPM and PERT, the 1960s saw an explosion of project-management tools and techniques. Here are a few:

- PERT/cost,[18] which introduced the work breakdown structure (WBS);
- RAMPS (resource allocation and multi-project scheduling);
- C/SCSC (cost/schedule control systems criteria);[19]
- earned value management,[20] which improved a project's ability to budget and subsequently manage its financial performance; and
- configuration management.

---

* Or "program management" for the Americans.
† Such as projects.

It didn't take long to rationalise these tools and techniques, and modern project management was well underway. In fact, except for risk management,10 modern project management hasn't substantially changed since the 1960s.

And now we come to software engineering. In 1968, the NATO Conference on Software Engineering was created to bring the theoretical foundations and practical disciplines from traditional engineering domains into the software world as a way to solve the so-called software crisis. The software crisis was a perception at the time[*] of the increasing inability of software development to deliver high-quality products in a timely manner — in general, attributed to the exponential rise in computing power.[21] Although there continues to be debate today as to whether there was a software crisis at all,[†] the participants at the conference concluded that there was definitely an identity crisis.[22]

In our opinion, this identity crisis was partly a "me too" attitude that came out of early software development — that software developers should have the same respect and reputation as engineers and others in "professions". This expressed itself in the idea that writing software should be predictable and mathematically provable like traditional engineering, akin to building a bridge. And so, in order to emulate engineering, software was wrapped up in projects with detailed requirements, specifications, and plans like any other engineering endeavour. Or that was the assumption — there was an idealised view of engineering disciplines amongst the NATO conference delegates that influenced many of the findings and recommendations.

But it did help. In many cases, this approach was able to bring discipline to large software projects and allow them to scale — but there was a high cost, which we will discuss in the next chapter.

With project management becoming a profession, industry certification bodies began to emerge; the most famous and relevant today would be the Project Management Institute (PMI), born in 1969.[2] That year also saw the emergence of the famous "iron triangle" metaphor for time, cost, and output in Martin Barnes's "Time and Money in Contract Control"[1] course.

Around this time, in August 1970, Royce first coined the term "waterfall"[23] in relation to projects for which each phase must be completed before the

---

[*] Which continues today.
[†] Or "is".

next starts. What is most interesting about this is that in that same paper, Royce acknowledged the significant risks of this approach:

> *I believe in this concept, but the implementation described above is risky and invites failure.... The testing phase which occurs at the end of the development cycle is the first event for which timing, storage, input/output transfers, etc., are experienced as distinguished from analyzed. These phenomena are not precisely analyzable.*

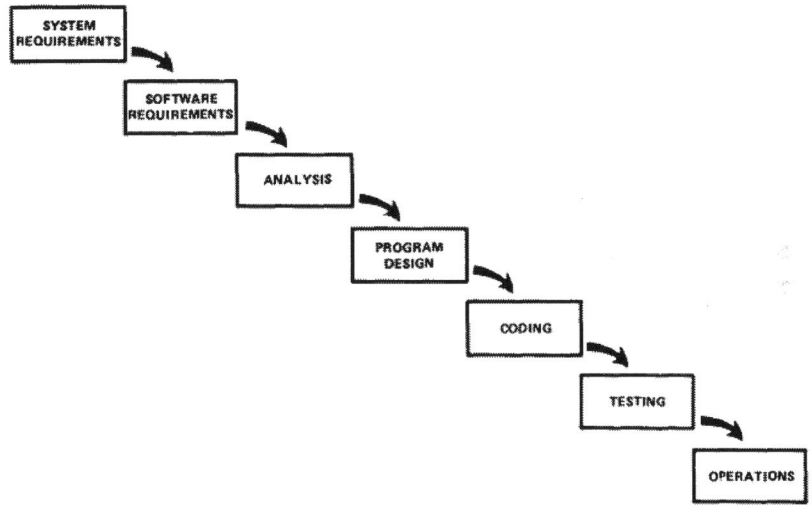

An idealised waterfall software project.[23]

Throughout the 1970s and 1980s, project management continued to consolidate its reputation as a profession and to position itself as a critical business process. The core responsibilities[*] expanded from simply managing time, cost, and scope to include risk management, stakeholder management, and quality management. Common project-management methods and frameworks were created and shared between companies — others, like PROMPT,[†] were commercialised.

Business models began to directly incorporate project management. Organisations began to use the capability maturity model (CMM) and, later, CMM integration (CMMI) to audit project-management maturity as part of their general process maturity. Industries began, incorrectly, to see software development as predictable and repeatable — a seemingly com-

---

* And associated processes and tools.
† Which would later become PRINCE2.

mon yet dangerous confusion between engineering and manufacturing. Watts Humphrey wrote in 1989:

Dr. W. E. Deming, in his work with the Japanese after World War II, applied the concepts of statistical process control to many of their industries. While there are important differences, these concepts are just as applicable to software as they are to producing consumer goods like cameras, television sets, or automobiles.[24]

As microcomputers became widely available to businesses, project-management software started to become more accessible.[19] The ease with which schedulers and project managers could schedule projects greatly simplified their jobs. This opened up project management to millions of smaller businesses but, on the downside, also gave the impression that anyone could run a project just by entering a list of tasks into a programme.[*]

The last 20 years has seen two major shifts in project management: a consolidation of frameworks and methods and a rise in agile project management. The consolidation has been strongly driven by PMI and the Project Management Body of Knowledge (PMBOK). If we look at the market share of different, non-agile project-management frameworks, the only real alternative to the PMBOK is the UK government's PRINCE2 ("PRojects IN a Controlled Environment") with 11% market share compared to PMI's 27%.[25] The vast majority continue to use ad hoc and custom project-management processes.

Agile project management emerged in the 1980s, although it didn't gain widespread market awareness until after the Agile Software Development Manifesto[26] was written in 2001. Agile itself isn't a framework or method, but rather is a value system used to deliver products in a highly flexible, customer-focused, incremental manner. There are hundreds of different agile frameworks, the most famous being Scrum[27], extreme programming (XP),[28] and Kanban.[29] It should be noted that most of these are not formal project-management frameworks;[†] rather, they are software-engineering practices or product-development methods. However, some frameworks, such as the DSDM agile project framework,[30] were specifically designed for this purpose. We assume that most readers have a passing familiarity with agile and we won't go into detail.

---

[*] I personally think Microsoft Project is singlehandedly responsible for the ruination of many projects and will probably be responsible for whatever project leads to the downfall of humanity — although Microsoft PowerPoint is a close second choice.

[†] Although many are (mis)used for this purpose.

Here's one interesting anecdote, however. The initial idea for Scrum was triggered by an HBR article from 1986 titled "The New New Product Development Game".[31] Note the term "product", not project. In fact, nothing in Scrum is designed for managing projects; rather, it is a product-development framework.

///

The Agile Manifesto

Written in 2001, the Manifesto for Agile Software Development[26] describes what it means to be agile:

We are uncovering better ways of developing software by doing it and helping others do it. Through this work we have come to value:

- *Individuals and interactions over processes and tools*
- *Working software over comprehensive documentation*
- *Customer collaboration over contract negotiation*
- *Responding to change over following a plan*

That is, while there is value in the items on the right, we value the items on the left more.

© 2001, the Agile Manifesto authors. This declaration may be freely copied in any form, but only in its entirety through this notice.

What do each of these values mean?

1. *We value individuals and interactions over processes and tools.* That is, while processes and tools can help sustain a consistent level of output, motivated individuals and teams collaborating and working together are more creative and can produce higher quality work.

2. *We value working software over comprehensive documentation.* This means that while processes that support delivery are important, the team's focus should be on delivering to the customer's needs.

3. *We value customer collaboration over contract negotiation.* Written contracts are still important. However, you should be treating your cus-

tomer as a partner, not as an opponent. The goal of an agile contract is to facilitate rather than protect, though it can do that as well.

4. *We value responding to change over following a plan.* Under agile, plans are useful as a guide, but adapting to your customer's changing requirements brings greater business value to both you and your customer.

The values on the right (processes, documentation, contracts, and plans) are still important; however, to be adaptable and agile, you need a greater appreciation of the values on the left (individuals, working software, customer collaboration, and responding to change).

upporting the four core values, are the 12 principles of the Agile Manifesto that define the agile mindset. These are the key attributes that are most important to agile practitioners. Keep in mind that, although originally written in the context of software engineering, the same mindset applies across almost any industry or domain.

1. *Our highest priority is to satisfy the customer through early and continuous delivery of valuable software.*
2. *Welcome changing requirements, even late in development. Agile processes harness change for the customer's competitive advantage.*
3. *Deliver working software frequently, from a couple of weeks to a couple of months, with a preference to the shorter timescale.*
4. *Business people and developers must work together daily.*
5. *Build projects around motivated individuals. Give them the environment and support they need, and trust them to get the job done.*
6. *The most efficient and effective method of conveying information to and within a development team is face-to-face conversation.*
7. *Working software is the primary measure of progress.*
8. *Agile processes promote sustainable development. The sponsors, developers, and users should be able to maintain a constant pace indefinitely.*
9. *Continuous attention to technical excellence and good design enhances agility.*
10. *Simplicity — the art of maximising the amount of work not done — is essential.*

11. *The best architectures, requirements, and designs emerge from self-organising teams.*

12. *At regular intervals, the team reflects on how to become more effective, then tunes and adjusts its behaviour accordingly.*

Which brings us to today. Project management is still evolving and can be best described as an "emerging profession".[10] It has brought significant standardisation to work models across the world;[32] you're likely to run projects the same way whether you are in Australia, the US, China, Japan, or Russia.

But we have a problem. The project way of working, as it's been evolving over the last few centuries, isn't keeping up with the needs of the modern economy — especially those businesses in the digital economy. But most organisations don't know anything else. Managers generally like projects because it gives them an answer to "When will it be done?" — or, more accurately, the perception of "when it will be done". The finance division also likes projects because they can encapsulate work in a neat little package, simplifying budgeting, forecasting, and financial management.

However, a lot of work in the modern economy is fundamentally ambiguous, unpredictable, and sometimes even chaotic. Projects nearly always go over time or over budget and someone is usually unhappy with any project that you run. Either the money runs out or the you deliver the product with fewer features and capability than the customer wants or the money continues and finance is unhappy because you're blowing their neat little 18-month forecast out of the water.

This is compounded by the fact that the development lifecycle of most products is much greater than that of the project (or "temporary endeavour") that initiated it. We're not talking about a construction project like a bridge: when the bridge is built, the bridge is built. There's no new customer value to be gained by continuing to work — you can't keep adding major features to a bridge. We're talking about knowledge work* where there is always more value to be created and where the maintenance cost is likely to be between two times[33] and 10 times[34] greater than the initial cost of bringing it to market. Even the fact that we are talking about total *cost* of ownership and not total *value* generated is indicative of the problem.

So where have projects gone wrong?

---

* Such as building software.

PART THREE

Where we went wrong

So where have projects gone wrong? In many ways, they haven't. Projects still have an important role to play in delivering time-critical and predictable work. The aforementioned bridge is only ever going to be delivered using a project. You're always going to need an up-front plan, a schedule, and a validated, approved architecture before beginning construction.

But a new culture is emerging amongst customers and organisations around the world: an expectation of continuous change and improvement. Most people would agree that the rate of change, and adoption of that change, has increased more in the last 40 years than in the previous 400. This is true in almost all aspects of our lives, from computers, cars, and communications to general consumer goods.[1] These days, we even change jobs almost as often as we change phones (every 4.2 years according to the US Department of Labour).[2]

The project mentality isn't keeping up with this changing pace of demand. We cannot fault the intention of an organisation when starting a project. The organisation identifies a need and, eventually, creates a project to address that need. But in this rapidly changing world, the needs of customers will change, outpace, and usually outlive a project's ability to deliver. How many times have you revisited the same product, project after project, to keep up with new demand? Therein lies the flaw, because that product isn't done. Thus, the core premise of a project, as a management construct with a fixed end that will deliver a complete product, is fundamentally flawed.[*]

And the flaw cuts deep because projects provide an illusion of predictability. One may go so far as to say a *delusion* of predictability. And we like predictability — it makes decisions easier, reduces the perception of risk, and provides confidence to leaders. It's also lazy management. As we'll see later in this chapter, projects in uncertain environments fail more often than not so the confidence placed in the promised predictability is misplaced.

---

[*] There has been a lot of discussion in the community about the word "projects". There's an argument that the word itself should be repurposed to incorporate any stream of product-development work, whether temporary or continuous. I actually like that idea. Most organisations already use the word incorrectly to describe any type of work and so, as part of the natural evolution of language, we can claim the word and redefine it for ourselves. However, for the purpose of clarity in this book, we'll keep to the formal definition.

That being said, projects do make sense for some cases: when the market is predictable and we can plan three, 12, or 24 months of work ahead of time. It's when the pace of change in the market exceeds the pace of change in our delivery that products and organisations fail. This is why startups, with their lower cost base and unbureaucratic delivery processes, often outperform established organisations. Those organisations that can embrace and leverage the unpredictable nature of the market generally do better.[3]

What this means to the way we deliver work is that if the product has untapped value for the customer, then organisations that can continuously deliver change can continuously meet new needs. Unfortunately, our overreliance on temporary projects, and the promise of predictability they provide, has led to a stagnation of thought; many organisations just don't know any other way to work. Hence #noprojects.

This continuous culture exposes another flaw in the project approach, one that is a lot more tangible: the cost of running a project. We're not talking about the cost to do the work, which occurs regardless of the operating model, but the (sometimes hidden) cost of running the project itself. By definition, projects are layers of management, governance, and supporting activities on top of an agreed sequence of work. Irrespective of the delivery model used (waterfall, iterative, or agile), these additional costs can be classified in three types, which we call the three O's: overhead, overrun, and opportunity costs.[4]

First, some quick definitions:

1. Overheads are the direct costs borne from running a project. These are relatively small, but the easiest to quantify and recover.
2. Overruns are potential costs that are realised when rectifying planning and estimation mistakes or overall project failure. Depending on the complexity of the work, the risk profile of the project, and the maturity of the organisation's estimation process, these costs can range from very small to very large.
3. An opportunity cost is the potential forgone revenue (or savings) between project initiation and completion. The longer a project runs without implementing a change, the larger the opportunity costs.

Let's start by agreeing that the overhead costs relating to the creation of value and delivery of outcomes will remain relatively constant regardless of the approach taken. In a software team, for example, costs unaffected by #noprojects include salaries and benefits of the developers during development activities (including testing and documentation), technical environments (e.g., development, test, staging, and production), continuous integration and delivery systems, licence fees, travel expenses, and office space for the team.*

However, by changing the delivery approach, #noprojects can negate many of the costs specifically related to managing a project. These include:

- project-specific events like kick-off meetings, project planning, and project closure;
- project-specific deliverables like milestone documents, sign-off packs, communication plans, schedules and Gantt charts, work plans, etc.;
- project administration, which may include staff hired to undertake project accounting or secretariat functions.
- project management offices (PMOs), which may include an organisation's PMO or smaller PMOs created at a programme level; and
- reduction in contractors and/or staff overtime because projects emphasise compliance to schedule, and many teams request overtime or hire additional contractors to meet estimated timelines.

Project managers are an interesting case. Removing projects doesn't necessarily mean removing project managers. As we will explore later, many of the skills of a project manager are still required and so we won't include them as overhead. You may find that these costs reduce, allowing individual project managers to spend their time on higher-value activities.†

We've known projects to spend more than six months in planning, chasing signatures and getting approvals for a two-month project. In other cases, we've seen project managers earn a salary over five times a developer's salary.‡ In these extreme cases, project overheads can actually exceed the cost of delivery.

We'll leave it to you to assess the potential overall cost savings for your organisation. However, to be realistic, you need to be able to distinguish between project overheads and common business overheads.

---

* In organisations with poor work practices, these costs may actually increase in the short term as a consequence of creating a mature work environment.
† Particularly in organisations that are over-governed or inefficient.
‡ And we're honestly not exaggerating.

We think it's safe to say that projects overrun and fail with disturbing regularity, whether by failing to deliver a solution that meets the business expectations, releasing later than planned, or costing more than initially budgeted. And the solution isn't better planning. Projects already spend significant energy in the early stages to plan and estimate the scale of effort and yet continue to have significant overruns. Note the alarming results from this study from the Harvard Business Review:[5]

> *We examined 1,471 projects, comparing their budgets and estimated performance benefits with the actual costs and results.... When we broke down the projects' cost overruns, what we found surprised us. The average overrun was 27% — but that figure masks a far more alarming one. Graphing the projects' budget overruns reveals a "fat tail" — a large number of gigantic overages. Fully one in six of the projects we studied was a black swan, with a cost overrun of 200%, on average, and a schedule overrun of almost 70%.*

These risks are compounded when there is undue pressure to align the project budget to a preconceived business expectation — which in turn leads to fuzzy estimates with little or no bearing on reality. Fundamentally, this leads to the question "why bother?"

What about #noestimates?

The #noestimates movement has been around longer than #noprojects, since about 2005,[6] and carries many of the same motivations although the two do not depend upon each other. When dealing with complex work that relies on human creativity and collaboration for completion, like building software or playing chess,[7] it will often take longer to try to figure out how long it will take than to just do the work. Johanna Rothman says that if the work is important enough to warrant doing then break it into small pieces, prioritize those pieces, start work on them, and predict when they will be done based on the actual rate of delivery rather than by guessing.[8] By ensuring that the work is prioritised, you learn quickly if it is worth doing, and you can easily change direction in response to feedback in the moment and ensure maximum value for effort. This book does not go deeply into #noestimates — others have already done that.[9]

What's even more concerning is that no matter how many projects we run, project failure rates remain consistent. A good example of this is the IT Project Success Rates Survey,[10] run by Scott Ambler since 2007. Accounting for the change in question in 2010, you can see that the change in success and failure rates has been insignificant (within 4%) from year to year.*

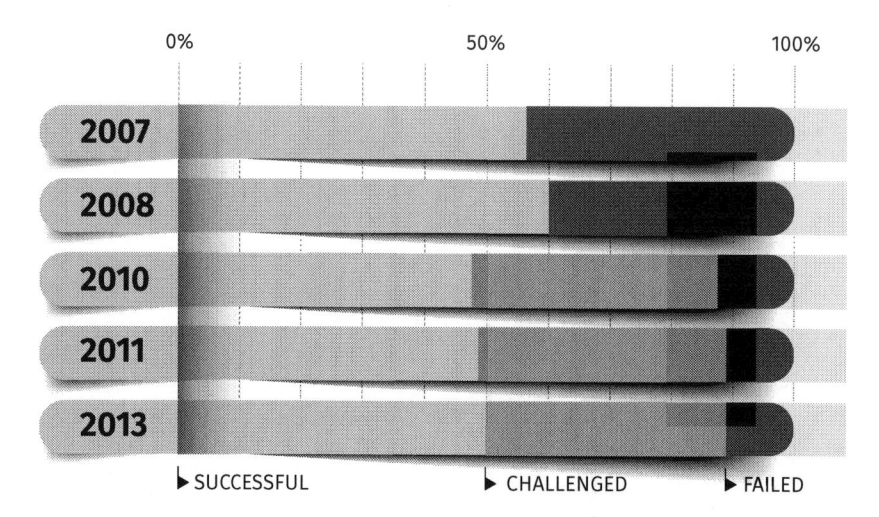

Comparison of project failure rates (non-agile) from 2007 to 2013.

These statistics are nothing new; you've probably seen some of them around. But that is exactly our point. IT project failure has become so commonplace that it is now accepted and usually expected. Read any project-management study and you'll see the spectre of project failure emerge. It's become such a joke that projects that actually deliver on time and on budget are a surprise.

Here are some more examples:

- A Geneca survey of 600 executives show that 75% of business and IT executives anticipate their software projects will fail and are "doomed right from the start".[11]
- The 2015 CHAOS survey shows that only 29% of all projects succeeded (delivered on time, on budget, with required features and functions), 52% were challenged (late, over budget, or with fewer than

---

* Another way to think about it is to do away with the traditional measurements that indicate failure (i.e., time, cost, and scope). Rather, success is about achieving outcomes and providing value — that's how we need to measure it.

the required features and functions), and 19% failed (cancelled prior to completion or delivered and never used).[12]

- EU figures for 214 technology projects from 1998 to 2005 showed that only one in eight technology projects met their time, budget, and quality objectives, with nearly 25% of all projects not completed at all. Total technology-project overruns in only 2004 totalled €142 billion.

- A 2010 KPMG survey showed that 70% of organisations had one or more failed projects during the previous 12 months.

- A 2008 survey by Logica showed that 35% of organisations abandoned a major project in the last three years.[13]

- Surveys of Harvard Business School's summer executive education programme provided examples of large IT failures that exceeded budgets by over 1,000%, from $30 million to $300 million, and only delivered 35% of requirements.[14]

In fact, when conducting the research for this last example, Harvard professors Rob Austin and Richard Nolan concluded that there were three dysfunctional elements prevalent in large IT projects:

1. The first flawed assumption is that it is actually possible to plan such a large project well enough that success is primarily determined by degree of conformance to a plan.

2. The second flawed assumption embedded in planning-intensive approaches is that it is possible to protect against late changes to a large system project.

3. The third flawed assumption is that it even makes sense to lock in big project decisions early.

This is easily backed up by the research from Watts Humphrey, who coined the requirements uncertainty principle: "The requirements will not be completely known until after the users have used the finished product."[15]

Agile projects don't get off easy either. Even agile projects, i.e., agile delivery wrapped inside a project structure, fail at a significant rate. A study by PMI[16] found that 75% of agile organisations met their goals, 65% completed on time, and 67% completed on budget. While this is still better than non-agile organisations (with 56%, 40%, and 45% respectively), a failure rate of one quarter to one third is still too high.

What about the return on investment? When a project runs over, can it still be considered a success? Sometimes yes, but unfortunately not in many cases. Based on findings from more than 5,400 IT projects, large IT projects run 45% over budget and 7% over time on average while delivering 56% less value than predicted. To quote McKinsey:

We also found that the longer a project is scheduled to last, the more likely it is that it will run over time and budget, with every additional year spent on the project increasing cost overruns by 15 percent.[17]

In fact, the project-management process is fundamentally designed to separate the work done from the business benefits. How many projects have you experienced that have claimed success (on time and on budget) but, after the project was closed and the project manager moved on, still failed to deliver the expected business benefits? There are too many in our experience.

By any criteria, an IT project has a significant risk of overrunning time, cost, or scope, with the associated financial, opportunity, and reputational costs. These statistics demonstrate a fundamental flaw in the approach taken to project management regardless of size, technology, vendor, approach, or processes used. Of most interest is that, in many cases, this is not a failure of the work but rather a failure of estimation and expectation. In reality, an activity takes as long as it takes — but that is usually longer than you want. The failure comes from wrapping a project construct around product delivery that is inappropriate for what you're trying to deliver.

They say that the definition of insanity is to do the same thing and expect a different result.* So why do organisations keep running projects?

#noprojects provides a less risky approach to delivery by removing the common factor in all of these failures: the project itself. This is not to say that there are no failures in a #noprojects approach. However, because of the continuous and discrete nature of #noprojects activities, failure is smaller, self-contained, and easily identified, and you can generally recover from it. Failure relating to project process, project governance, stakeholder buy-in, and scope management becomes, by definition, far less likely.

---

* This quote is commonly attributed to Einstein, but there is no evidence that he actually said it.

Opportunity costs and the cost of delay[18] can be the hardest to quantify but also can be the largest costs to an organisation running a project. As mentioned earlier, we have seen organisations take up to six months of planning and approvals just to begin a two-month project. That's six months of forgone revenue or productivity gains. We're not even going to begin to get into the cost of locking in a specific option at the expense of any other option. With a #noprojects approach, you are able to bring value to market sooner and adapt to market changes faster than you could had you initiated a traditional project.

Organisations that can calculate the cost of delay are better placed to appropriately prioritise work and reduce their internal bureaucracy in order to make optimal decisions. In many cases, the organisation's own design is the culprit. We have seen divisions spend months negotiating to transfer budget from one to another* in order to fund a project that everyone agreed was absolutely critical. And this almost always leads to significant project overruns.

Even if you can't make quantitative calculations, it's possible to assess the cost of delay in a qualitative manner. Joshua Arnold[19] writes that the cost of delay has two essential ingredients: value (defined as killer, bonus, or meh) and urgency (defined as ASAP, soon, or whenever). An idea that is killer and needed ASAP is likely to have a very high cost of delay per week.

---

*   Even though they are on the same P&L sheet.

Qualitative Cost of Delay

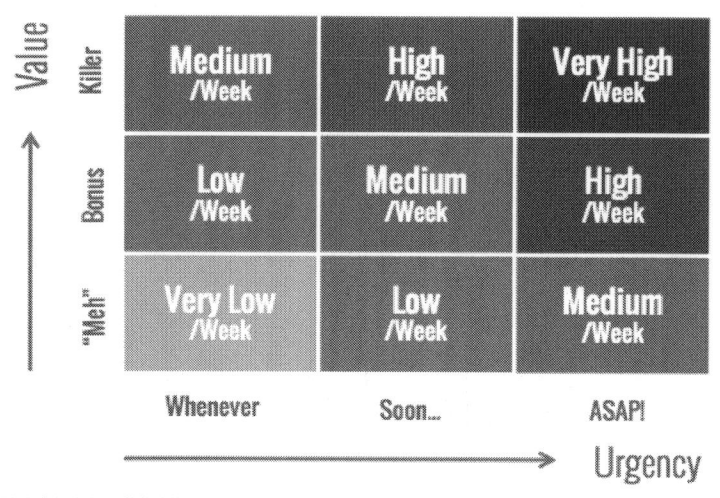

Value	Whenever	Soon...	ASAP!
Killer	Medium/Week	High/Week	Very High/Week
Bonus	Low/Week	Medium/Week	High/Week
"Meh"	Very Low/Week	Low/Week	Medium/Week

→ Urgency

BLACK SWAN FARMING

Qualitative cost of delay.

Once again, we can turn to reports and research for actual examples of this. In 2008, the US Treasury Inspector General for Tax Administration released audit findings of the delayed Electronic Fraud Detection System project. In its own words, "we estimated that during PY 2006, when the fraud detection system was not operational, the IRS failed to stop approximately $894 million in fraudulent refunds."[20]

And this is just the forgone revenue. It doesn't include the direct costs borne by the organisation for workarounds, interest on that forgone revenue, or revenue from any potential reinvestment.

When looking at other opportunity costs, you would also consider:
- lost market share,
- flow-on costs to customers,
- continuing maintenance costs for legacy systems, and
- productivity loss (or, more accurately, unrealised productivity gain).

We feel that this quote from Johanna Rothman perfectly encapsulates this idea:

Johanna, we want to ship this product in the second quarter this year. We estimate it will take us a quarter to ramp up sales. We think there are lifetime sales of about five years for this product. Any delays in our shipment will not push our sales figures to the right. They will remove our max sales from the middle. Got it? We have to make our ship date.[21]

Agile delivery doesn't help here. In the majority of cases, the overhead occurs at the start of a project when project approval and funding processes drive the associated opportunity costs. Ask yourself if the confidence you gain from writing all those business cases, stakeholder and communication strategies, RACI matrices, project plans, schedules, and endless approval meetings is really worth more than the cost of delay.* How much governance is enough and how much do you really need?

Incremental and agile delivery methods can help once work has started but are of limited help during project initiation. And as any process is only as fast as its slowest point, these early delays and bottlenecks can have significant flow-on impacts to the rest of the project.

This is all symptomatic of the project mentality, where projects cause organisations to focus on the work rather than on what's important to an organisation or customer. The best example we have comes from a project-management guide that we found as we were researching for this book:

While the reason for undertaking a project may have been to reduce utility costs by 10% or to increase productivity by 20%, achieving such goals may be outside the scope of the project.[22]

This is the problem. Projects are decoupling delivery from value. And to be fair, there's a reason for it — it's much simpler to measure an output than an outcome. If you need to decide whether to pay for something, asking "how much does it cost?" is a lot easier to answer than "what is it worth?" And because your financial measurement systems focus on what is measurable rather than what is valuable, you tend to be biased towards perceived efficiency† at the expense of improving productivity.

Irrespective of the delivery model used (waterfall, iterative, or agile), projects are not working well. They increase the total cost of ownership and reduce return on investment. They introduce additional risk and cost for a false sense of predictability, just to give leaders comfort.

---

* If it's not obvious, we don't think they are. :-)
† A term more polite than "cutting costs".

The answer is not "do better projects" — we have been trying to do better projects for 400 years. This approach has led to highly optimised project-management processes that have improved how you deliver the easily measured outputs rather than the valuable outcomes. So, if better projects are not the solution, then perhaps a solution is to not do projects at all. #noprojects brings a different viewpoint and an alternative way of looking at work, focusing first and foremost on business outcomes while delivering work as a continuous stream of value rather than a temporary endeavour.

PART FOUR

Outcomes over outputs

About 10 years ago, Evan was the programme manager responsible for delivering a government system to map the Australian national population against various government statistics (such as socio-demographic census data, health-care spending, and government infrastructure spending). The theory was that by mapping this data to locations, we could better help the government identify areas of disadvantage and focus spending, which is a reasonable goal.

But before we talk about the outcomes, let's start at the beginning. The business case was long* and we spent a lot of time finding "benefits". We have put benefits in quotes because the funding had already been assigned (as part of the annual government funding processes) before we wrote the project business cases. But we had to find benefits before finance would release the funds. After a few months of back and forth, we found the description of benefits that made finance happy. But it didn't matter; we had a great idea and it looked good. Sound familiar?

We spent many millions of dollars over four years. We released new functionality every month (it was an agile project). We set business milestones: we met some and missed some, but we hit most of the quantifiable benefits and overall the organisation was happy with what we delivered. By all definitions it was a successful project — but what happened to it?

Nothing at all. By the time Evan left the project, we had maybe 100 users and, as far as we could tell, very few of them actually used the tool to inform where to focus spending. We probably would have had a better outcome if we'd just given each user $10,000 to invest in their programmes.

This is the problem. In most companies, the focus on successfully delivering projects has distanced them from focusing on delivering value to their customers. And it should not be controversial to say that delivering value is an organisation's *raison d'être,* and work that does not create value should be avoided. All too often, organisations have been measuring activity and cost instead of outcomes and value — our argument is that organisations need to change this to remain competitive.

In the example above, we started with the idea for a product, then we found the benefits and outcomes. If we knew then what we know now, we would have ignored the product and started purely from the outcome. And everything we did from there should have been focused on that. We might never have created the sexy product that everyone asked for, but we might have produced something that everyone used.

---

* I (Evan) know, because I wrote much of it.

So, by focusing on the project, we lost sight of the product. And by focusing on the product, we lost sight of the value.

And that's what #noprojects is all about: the alignment of activities to outcomes, measured by value, constrained by guiding principles, and (optionally) supported by continuous-delivery technologies.[1] It's about continuous delivery. It's about moving away from a finite construct of fixed outputs and fixed timeframes and moving towards a model of "we have a product and we're going to develop the product only until it makes sense to stop developing the product". It's about changing our measurements and monitoring processes from measuring outputs to measuring outcomes, about looking at value realisation rather than lines of code, requirements, or user stories met.

But before we go any further, let's start with some basic #noprojects terminology.

An **outcome** is a meaningful, and fundamental, change in the status quo as a result of some work.[*] Intended and actual outcomes should be expressed in measurable terms. There are four types of outcomes:
1. good and intended,
2. good and unintended,
3. bad and unintended, and
4. bad and intended.

We are talking about mainly number 1 and occasionally number 4, and we hope to use rapid feedback cycles and the continuous culture (to be discussed in much more detail in later chapters) to expose number 2 and avoid or minimise number 3.

Value is the often-intangible change that is the result of work and contributes to achieving an outcome.[†]

A **portfolio** is the prioritised backlog of work underway or to be done. It includes building new products or services, maintaining existing products or services, and business-as-usual (BAU) activities.

An **activity** is any discrete piece of work that is undertaken as part of a change.

---

[*] Some organisations may use the term "benefits" and "outcomes" interchangeably. The two concepts are closely aligned and, for the purpose of this book, we have chosen to predominantly use the term outcomes.

[†] Value is the subject of the next chapter and its case study.

As we move away from temporary project teams, team permanence becomes a necessity. The **value-delivery team** is a dedicated, stable, and cross-functional team (or network of teams) accountable for an outcome.

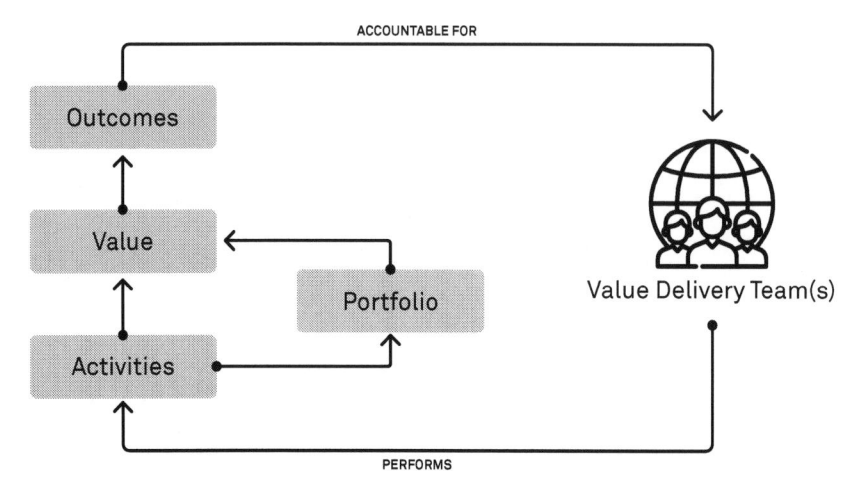

The relationship between value-delivery teams, activities, the portfolio, value, and outcomes.*

This relationship could be described thus: you need to justify work based on the value it could deliver to the organisation in the context of a business outcome. That is a simple sentence, but the relationship between outcomes, value, and work is at best complex and often chaotic — it is very hard to link a specific piece of work directly to a specific outcome. Instead, look at the trend of value generated from multiple activities over a period of time. In many businesses, committing to specific value from specific work is a dangerous, but common, behaviour.

The first step to understand the relationship between work and outcomes is understanding complexity theory. The Cynefin framework is a tool for making sense of a domain and describes the inherent nature of the work needed to address a problem or opportunity.

---

* This is a deliberately simplified view of the relationships. The reality includes some level of coordination between delivery teams, particularly in situations where multiple value-delivery teams need to collaborate to achieve an outcome. See the conversation about the value-management office in a later chapter.

Cynefin explained

Cynefin[2] is a Welsh word that roughly translates as "the place of our being". It is the term Dave Snowden uses to describe a way of understanding and responding to complexity in a domain. He presents the following diagram to show the different aspects of complexity:

Each of the domains in the model has characteristics that indicate ways to work or to respond when working in that state. Snowden points out that this is not a two-dimensional consulting model but is a sense-making tool used to determine the most appropriate type of response to take when acting in a specific domain.

The five domains of Cynefin (CC-BY-SA Dave Snowden)

We use the model to select the approach to use to solve a problem or to take advantage of an opportunity in a business setting.

Let's look at the first four domains, starting from the lower right corner.

Obvious: The nature of the problem is clear to all concerned and how to solve the problem is well understood. Obvious problems are ones that have been solved many times before and there are genuine best-practice approaches to use to solve the problem. It may not be easy, but there are rules to follow, and when they are followed, the problem will be solved. Activities such as civil engineering or construction (e.g., building all the houses in a new subdivision) often fall into the Obvious domain. Plan the work in detail then follow the plan precisely.

Complicated: The problem is relatively clear to all concerned and there is a well-understood outcome to aim for, but how to get there is not obvious. In this domain, the key is to identify the combination of good practices that align with achieving the outcome. There may be a need to learn and adapt along the path, but the intended result is clear to all concerned. Building computer systems to address known business problems falls into this category: there is a wide range of possible approaches that could be taken, there will be a lot of learning as the solution evolves, and the link between the solution and the problem is relatively clear. Agile development methods with their focus on strong technical practices and rapid feedback will often be appropriate in this domain.

Complex: The relationship between problem/opportunity and solution is not clear and there is a need to experiment to uncover the actual problem. You can undertake many parallel experiments, and there is a need to run those experiments rapidly and at low cost. The ideas of lean startup (build-measure-learn) are well suited to this domain. Run a small experiment, check the results, and either amplify the solution with the next experiment or pivot and run an experiment with a different focus. The intent is to experiment and learn in order to clarify the underlying problem/opportunity (in which case the problem moves to the Complicated domain and the experimentation can give way to more structured learning) or to come to the realisation that the problem/opportunity should be abandoned.

Chaotic: There is no discernible relationship between cause and effect, between problem and solution. In this state, there is no clear vision of what you need to do to address the problem, and the solutions will not be evident until after they emerge. It is important to act quickly as chaos states will devolve into more and more chaos, but exactly what actions will solve the problem are not clearly discernible. Firefighting is an example of a chaotic domain — doing nothing is not an option but exactly what needs to be done is often not directly visible to all concerned, and often the act of addressing the problem will cause other problems (e.g., water damage in parts of a building that did not burn).

Kurtz and Snowden provide an example of the impact of trying to apply ordered thinking in the Chaotic or Complex domains:

> *A group of West Point graduates were asked to manage the playtime of a kindergarten as a final year assignment. The cruel thing is that they were given time to prepare. They planned; they rationally identified objectives; they determined backup and response plans. They then tried to "order" children's play based on rational design principles, and, in consequence, achieved chaos. They then observed what teachers do. Experienced teachers allow a degree of freedom at the start of the session, then*

intervene to stabilize desirable patterns and destabilize undesirable ones; and, when they are very clever, they seed the space so that the patterns they want are more likely to emerge. [3]

A fifth domain, **Disorder**, sits in the centre of the model and is the state that any system must go through when moving from one domain to another.

The cliff-face symbology between Obvious and Chaotic is intended to indicate the risk (perhaps, the likelihood) that Obvious domains can quickly become Chaotic if the rules by which they are working become invalid due to some external or internal influence.

In addition to the five domains, the model has what Snowden calls "liminal" areas on the boundary of Complicated and Complex and the boundary of Complex and Chaotic. In the liminal spaces, there is lots of learning and experimentation to do to identify the best approach to tackling the problem.

In the Complex/Complicated liminal area, Snowden recommends experimentation using prototypes and iterations. For the Complex/Chaotic liminal area, he talks about the need to abandon constraints to allow novelty to emerge.[4]

So, when looking at any opportunity to invest, you need to understand the likely nature of the work that will be needed to take advantage of the opportunity. Where the work is clear and the value generation is obvious (an obvious system), then any delivery model, including traditional projects, is appropriate. The more abstract the value generation from the work, the more you enter the territory of complicated, complex, or even chaotic systems. By their nature, projects do not operate well in these environments.

Back to the topic at hand. Whether at the level of team, division, or organisation, the continuous flow of activities is focused on changing **outcomes** (the benefits realised as a result of work) rather than **outputs** (the product of the work).[5] An outcome is measured by its value to the organisation, whether direct and tangible or indirect and intangible. Outcomes are planned, slowly changing, and define the common direction for the organisation.*

How's this different from a project? Assume that we run a HR division. Our outcome, or one of our outcomes, is staff retention. That's our rationale; that's why we exist. We create a team whose job, whose only job, is to improve or maintain staff retention. That's what they are accountable for. The actual products or activities that we do are the outputs, the means to the end. As long as what we do remains within our budget and improves staff retention, we can choose to spend our budget however we like. While there is value to be created, the team continues to operate.

Understand though, that outcomes can be complex, interdependent, and occasionally conflicting. To effectively manage this at an organisation level, you need to understand four things:

1. the profile of the outcome,
2. the relationship between outcomes,
3. the principles that align work across all outcomes, and
4. the impact of unintended consequences.

The profile of an outcome defines the context, intent, and expectations for the team, division, or organisation. While the characteristics of a profile will differ between organisations, at a minimum it should contain the following:

1. **Summary** — This is a short description of the outcome.

2. **Owner** — Who (either an individual or team) is accountable for this outcome?

3. **Measurement** — If the outcome is quantifiable,† how do you measure it? How will you measure effectiveness of the activities against the outcome target?

4. **Current** baseline — What is the current state of the measure?

5. **Current target** — What are you trying to achieve? Try to avoid percentages‡ and remember that this is a *current* target. It will change

---

* Here's a hint to get you started: determine the specific (measurable) impact that the work you are doing today has against key business outcomes. If you can start here, this will greatly smooth out the transition away from projects.
† And most should be.
‡ As they can be easily gamed.

over time. Depending on the context of the outcome, the current target may also have a timeframe or due date.

6. **Cadence** — How frequently will you be measuring the outcome? Automatic measures (those which can be calculated without human intervention) should be done as regularly as reasonable. Those which require polls or surveys of users or team members should be scheduled to avoid overload.

7. **Lag/lead time** — How soon after doing work will you see the effect on the outcome?

8. **Dependencies and order (ranking)** — Where does this outcome sit in relation to your other outcomes?

9. **Budget** — What is your maximum available investment/budget to achieve this outcome?

What is *not* included in the profile is a plan. The team is expected to dynamically react and pro-act* to opportunities in the market or organisation by instituting continuous change.

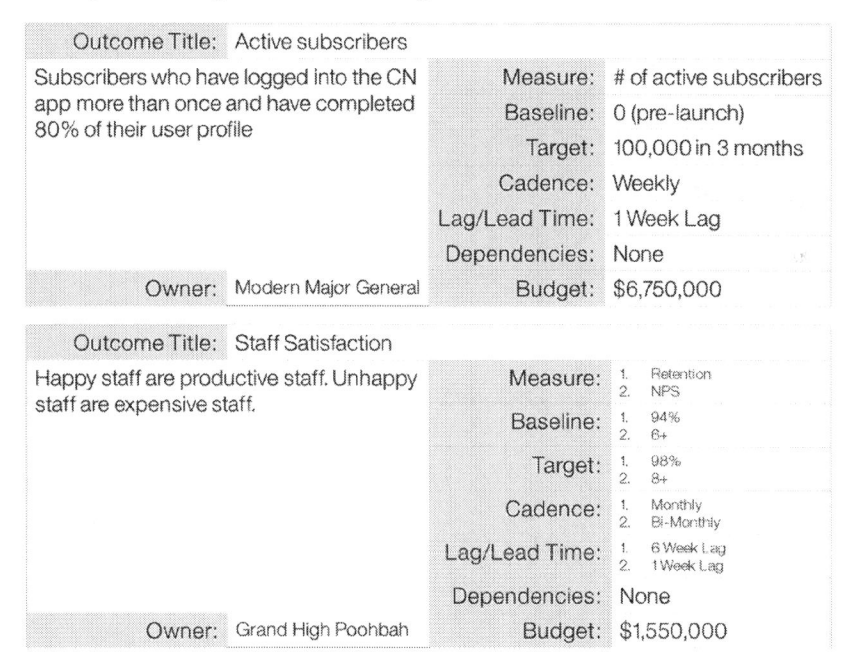

Outcome Title:	Active subscribers		
Subscribers who have logged into the CN app more than once and have completed 80% of their user profile		Measure:	# of active subscribers
		Baseline:	0 (pre-launch)
		Target:	100,000 in 3 months
		Cadence:	Weekly
		Lag/Lead Time:	1 Week Lag
		Dependencies:	None
Owner:	Modern Major General	Budget:	$6,750,000

Outcome Title:	Staff Satisfaction		
Happy staff are productive staff. Unhappy staff are expensive staff.		Measure:	1. Retention 2. NPS
		Baseline:	1. 94% 2. 6+
		Target:	1. 98% 2. 8+
		Cadence:	1. Monthly 2. Bi-Monthly
		Lag/Lead Time:	1. 6 Week Lag 2. 1 Week Lag
		Dependencies:	None
Owner:	Grand High Poohbah	Budget:	$1,550,000

Sample outcome profiles for a mid-sized product company.

---

* If that's not a word, it should be.

Getting to the real business outcomes for an organisation (or team) may seem simple but it can be very difficult in reality. Worse still, there is an easy answer — but it's wrong. A lot of organisations will define their outcomes around money — either revenue, signings, or profit. "We need to increase our quarterly profit by 17%" or "our target is to sign 20 new clients" or "we need to make $10 million in revenue this quarter". While these statements may be true, they are not business outcomes.

You are not in business to make money. We'll say that again: **You are not in business to make money.**[*] That is not your purpose. If you're focusing on making money, you're not focusing on creating value for your customer. Think of your local doctor — most have not become a doctor to make money. They become doctors to save lives. They make money in order to continue saving lives.

Frederic Laloux said, "Profit is like the air we breathe. We need air to live, but we don't live to breathe."[6]

So, while remembering that you still need to make money and be profitable, what are your business outcomes? No book can answer that question for you, but there are some simple practices to help you to discover it.

The most common practice available is called "5 Whys". It's simple cause-and-effect interrogation technique borrowed from the Toyota Production System and lean manufacturing.[7] Start by looking at the work that you do for your customer. Now ask "why?" "Why do we do this?" or "why do we need this?" Then, use your answer as the basis for the next question: ask "why?" again.[†] Asking "why?" five times is, anecdotally, sufficient to get to the root outcome. And you'll be able to get there in fewer steps in many cases.

If your answer is "to make money", you've gone too deep and abstracted it to the point of meaninglessness. Everyone needs to make money — there's no differentiation from your competitors in that. Making money is how you show that you are actually solving that need. It's a measure or an indicator, not the reason. Go back up a level. That's your outcome.

Repeating the process from different perspectives and exploring new answers to "why" can help you discover multiple root outcomes. Likewise,

---

[*] And a third time for luck. You are not in the business of making money. (Okay… if you're an investment bank then you are in the business of making money, but that's not true for other organisations.)

[†] While really annoying in my five-year old, it's an incredibly powerful technique.

if you come to a looping question/answer series or highly generalised statements (such as money or satisfaction), you should look at rephrasing the "why" question to uncover new lines of inquiry. We also find that external, impartial facilitation can help to uncover real root outcomes and avoid confirmation biases and "we've always done it this way" syndrome.

There is a natural granularity to outcomes at different levels — organisational, divisional, and team. At an organisational level, outcomes are generally broad and focused on multiple customers, internal staff, and work processes.

Divisional outcomes are generally a natural decomposition of a single organisational outcome. The intent of this decomposition is to provide focus and ownership of the outcome within the organisation. Accountability will often sit with a senior executive, e.g., the CIO, CMO, or CFO.

At a team level, outcomes are highly specific and should relate to the divisional outcomes. However, given the natural complexity in organisational structures, team level outcomes may also have secondary parent outcomes.

For example, these are potential outcomes for a startup company:

- **Organisational outcome** — Sell the company for $X per share while guaranteeing jobs for 80% of existing staff.

- **Divisional outcome** — Increase revenue from subscriptions to $X per quarter.

- **Team outcome** — Increase the conversion rate from free to paid accounts to 2%.

To be effective in the long term, outcomes need to be constrained. You can't let divisions and teams do anything they want unchecked. At the same time, you can't significantly restrict their ability to deliver. To reconcile those requirements, create a set of ranked principles: rules that apply to all activities regardless of outcome. It is expected that every organisation will create their own principles depending on what is important to them. Principles may constrain a team in areas of quality, communication, staff engagement, security, branding, or any other common area.

Be aware that each principle brings with it an increase in cost and effort for every activity. For this reason, principles are given a ranking. You can use any prioritisation model, but we generally recommend MoSCoW:

- **Must have (M)** — non-negotiable principles that every activity must comply with in order to be considered done, without exception. Examples: All activities **must** have associated automated unit tests written prior to development commencing (TDD); before opening an account, a customer **must** provide at least three forms of identification, one of which **must** be a government-issued identity card with photograph.

- **Should have (S)** — teams need to comply with these principles or justify their non-compliance. Examples: All authentication **should** link directly to the corporate Active Directory system; mortgages **should** only be issued for 80% of the value of the property used as collateral.

- **Could have (C)** — optional principles that act as guidelines at the discretion of the team. Examples: OWASP security tests **could** be written for each activity and run as part of the regression test suite; we **could** ask customers to provide up to four telephone numbers as contacts.

- **Won't have (W)** — negative principles that teams should avoid.

The largest risks to this way of working are conflicting outcomes and the unintended consequences they cause. Outcomes can conflict when there is poor communication and collaboration between divisions or teams, a lack of clarity in describing outcomes, or conflicting priorities between distinct outcomes. They can also conflict due to the natural tension between growth/change and stability/status quo.

These unintended consequences can be mitigated in five ways:

1. **Active and adaptive portfolio management** — Larger organisations can manage a list of major ideas, aligned by business outcome and ranked. Teams can then pull initiatives when they have capacity, rather than forming temporary teams around work.

2. **A publicly available activity canvas** — When the activity canvas of each team is visible to the entire organisation, teams validate that other activities will not negatively impact them. This requires teams to actively check the activity canvas of closely related teams. However, it is still important to promote transparency and clarify any changes that may cause a negative impact.

3. **Keep teams stable yet share knowledge** — There is a strong evidence of the benefits of keeping teams together for extended periods of time. There is also value in sharing knowledge and skills across teams by rotating people. The difficulty lies in balancing these contradictory needs, yet that balance of stability and sharing is critically important. "At a software services firm, a 50% increase in team familiarity was followed by a 19% decrease in defects and a 30% decrease in deviations from budget. On audit and consulting teams, high familiarity yielded a 10% improvement in performance, as judged by clients."[8]

4. **Professionalism and pride in work** — Whatever the nature of the work, team members must hold themselves to a high technical standard. This does not mean being a team of experts, but teams are expected to work to a high standard and take pride in the work that they do. From a software standpoint, for instance, this means that we resolve technical debt as soon as reasonable.

5. **Working principles** — Finally, the identification and development of each activity needs to comply with the agreed-upon working principles. This ensures that changes that lead to short-term gains don't lead to larger issues in the longer term.

Without binding a team to a specific output, an organisation that understands and plans for growth outcomes can fundamentally adapt to a changing market. Governance controls come in the form of common working principles and clearly defined, non-conflicting outcomes. In this way, senior management can delegate the "how" to their value-delivery teams while retaining ownership of the "what" and "why".

CASE STUDY

Shipping is NOT success - let it sail!

by Naresh Jain

All organisations, from the largest enterprise to the newest startup, face the same challenge: how to solve their users' problems by bringing a superior product (or service) to market faster than their competitors while reducing effort spent on overhead activities or, worse, building the wrong product. I hope no one wants to build "stuff" for the sake of being busy.

This is especially critical in organisations that produce consumer products. My case study describes how one such organisation, building products used by millions of diverse users every day, used a #noprojects and #noestimates approach to meet this challenge.

Problems

In any organisation, understanding your user is always difficult. And this is compounded for consumer products with millions of diverse users, each with their own reasons for using the product. In our case, we had three distinct problems:

1. How do we build a novel product that appeals to our entire user base without making it too complex or expensive (both to build and to maintain)?

2. How do we find the right user needs to focus on and make the right feature decisions (with the best ROI)?

3. How do we innovate rapidly and build a superior product faster than our competitors (improve the time to market and reduce friction)?

While we had a good start with millions of happy users and big investors, we were also exposed to stiff competition from some of the most innovative global tech giants. To beat them, we had to up our game.

Causes

The company founder hired a new executive from the Valley. The new hire started to question some of the decisions that had been made: "How many features did we build last year? What was the traction of those features?"

That is not to say that the company wasn't already asking those questions, but a fresh perspective was a strong reminder that they needed to critically examine the product. When they looked at the data, they saw that they had shipped hundreds of features in the previous year, but many of them weren't being used as widely as they had wished. The teams were super productive in shipping but not in generating engagement. They were too eager to celebrate success as soon as they shipped. They produced a lot of waste in the process.

There had to be a better way. This was the state when I joined the organisation.

Solution

Our solution had five key elements:

1. We structured teams around user-first product thinking rather than platforms or functions. We called these "value teams" — each responsible for a specific end-to-end user experience (or theme) and consisting of people with the skills necessary to deliver the result. Because user experience is common across platforms, we needed everyone, from mobile to web, to work together. This also meant completely changing how we managed the product roadmap, planned team capacity, and measured effectiveness.

2. We changed our organisational metrics to focus on nine key OKRs, which we gradually reduced to just three, centred on user engagement, user retention, and how deeply the user is invested in our product. Even that wasn't going far enough — about five months into the journey, we realized that even three were too many. We gave each value team one primary OKR that they had to actively improve and two secondary OKRs that they had to maintain at least at the same level.

3. We focused on building a learning organisation and building skills and talent (through both acquisition and improvement). We focused on craftsmanship and developing mastery in all disciplines. We also tried to create cross-functional teams by embedding dedicated designers, testers, data analysts, and user-insight people in each value team.

4. We decentralised portfolio management and used a simple data-driven governance model to decide how much to invest in which value team. We killed all discussion of prioritisation, estimation, and resource allocation while shifting the focus to value and impact. Each team could statistically show their impact and decide things appropriately.

5. We moved all teams towards a continuous-discovery and continuous-delivery culture. We started with a problem hypothesis and validating the same with user data. We'd come up with three solution hypotheses and determine the best fit of these by testing them on users. We'd take the winner and run a slice of it in an A/B test with 1% of our users. We used data to decide if we'd refine, scale, pivot, or scrap the idea.

Let me explain how this worked. We had a team that was responsible for the onboarding experience — everything (on every platform) that a new user experiences in the first 24 hours. Another team was responsible for the payments experience. And yet another team was responsible for the third-party-partner experience. We created 12 value teams — although, over a year, we killed six of them and added two new teams as we learned what worked and what did not.

An important consideration was how to measure the impact of each team and how to identify a team that may need more leadership support. This needed us to shift away from output-centric measurements toward measuring outcomes and impact — and to get our teams to understand impact and outcomes. We spent the better part of a month designing what we thought would be a good set of universal measures and defining what good outcomes mean.

It was important to build the right culture. And because we believe that culture emerges from structure, it is important that these teams truly owned the end-to-end experience and could go deep into it to connect with the user experience and the user psychology.

When I describe it like this, it might sound like we started with a clear idea about how everything would work. In reality, it was a lot messier. It took a year of experimentation and adaptation to come up with this solution.

Implementation

The first thing that we did was to challenge how product decisions were being made. We moved from gut feelings or pseudo data-driven (biased) decision making to using statistically significant user data to make informed decisions. We made a significant investment in democratising data and running experiments at scale, which could help everyone in the company to gain insight from data and make more informed decisions. Anyone could challenge the product manager if the data did not support the hypothesis.

The other big challenge was the number of long-term bets that the company had been focusing on. In order to keep the board and the investors happy, we had to have grand things to talk about. Many times, these big, new, shiny things would take over. Breaking those big ideas into tangible, quantifiable experiments was really important. Putting a WIP limit on these long-term bets was equally important as we were seeing a significant impact from refining and polishing what we already had. The balance is extremely critical.

Once we started down this path, two things emerged:

1. Our annual plan focused on fewer big bets and featured a lot of emergent short-term bets (refinements). This meant that the teams could be lot more responsive to users, as they learned about user behaviour and measured usage patterns without having to worry about the big bets.

2. This also meant that we could move out of marketing-driven-development mode — i.e., marketing was no longer calling the shots on the timeline. This led to teams feeling less pressure to deliver. They could really experiment and iterate ideas in a safe-to-fail environment. We would prove with data that a hypothesis worked on a statistically significant chunk of the user base before we rolled it out to the entire user base. Marketing also become an integral part of our day-to-day activities, giving teams more confidence in this approach. Now, our teams were able to focus on the core user need and give users a "wow" experience.

This directly led to thinking that we could structure work around self-contained themes, thus allowing teams to own the full end-user experience. We called these "value teams".

Unlike earlier project teams, these value teams were permanent. We brought together cross-functional skills and encouraged the teams to deeply examine user psychology. We needed them to understand user needs so that they could design a product that would glue our users to their screens for 12 hours a day.

This was a fundamental shift in how the organisation operated — shifting from project-based thinking, with all its associated overhead and short-term perspective, to product-based thinking from a user's point of view.

Even the makeup of the teams changed. We had:
- a product manager,
- a data analyst,
- a designer,
- a tech lead,
- iOS developers,
- Android developers,
- Windows developers,
- back-end microservices developers,
- a user-insight (CI) person (folks that reach out to users for feedback and user intelligence), and
- theme testers (integration testers would essentially look at the entire product across all the teams).

You'll notice that we didn't have an ops person in the team — we taught the developers to take on this responsibility.

Challenges

There was a lot of experimentation and volatility throughout our journey. We could categorise what we learned as team design, politics, and measurement.

We spent a lot of time experimenting with team design. We started by creating 12 teams, which we then dropped to eight, then to six. We ended up going back to eight. This volatility was natural as we were clearly measuring the impact each team/theme had on the broader business outcomes. Themes that didn't have a material impact on the OKRs we either dismantled or restructured and reassigned those people so there was no fear of job loss, which allowed the teams to be honest and not game the metrics.

We had the usual challenge of managers who felt that they were losing control. Historically, they'd build up political capital based on team size, and we took that into account when forming (and re-forming) teams.

Our biggest challenge was measurements and metrics. Historically, we tended to try to micro-measure things. We generally thought that the more we measure something and the more precisely we measure it, the better we got at understanding it. But the opposite was true. At the time, we were measuring NPS and several other misleading KPIs, but all we were really doing was feeding our own confirmation biases — the more data we had, the more we could make that data say what we wanted it to.

Once we decided that increasing engagement and retention was our target OKR (and I'd go so far as to say that that target is relevant for every company), we needed to decide how to measure it. We commissioned our data-science team to look at groups of highly engaged users to find their "aha!" moment and distil that into something we could measure. We discovered some interesting correlations between various behaviours and usage patterns that allowed us to refine our impact measurements.

We ended up using this information proactively to improve user engagement and retention. It also helped everyone in the company focus on the same impact and talk the same language. These are important ingredients for creating a user-first thinking culture.

Outcome

We achieved some pretty fantastic outcomes. User retention rose by over 20% and engagement rose by over 30%. While it took us longer than before to release features, when we did release, we had much better conversions. Without spending a single penny on marketing campaigns, we had a steady flow of new users coming in. And, most importantly, the culture changed as well. We are now more likely to experiment and kill new features than ship and fail.

The journey continues. While I'm not involved with this company anymore, they continue to evolve their business structures and models to meet the changing demands of their users.

PART FIVE

Value over busy

Which brings us to value.... The Oxford English Dictionary[1] defines value as "the regard that something is held to deserve; the importance, worth, or usefulness of something" and "the worth of something compared to the price paid or asked for it".

Outcomes are only achieved when work delivers something of value, and the intent of all work is to generate direct or indirect value. However, value is a nebulous and abstract term — if you ask 20 people what value means to them, you will get 30 different answers. Regardless, for the purposes of this book, an exact definition of value doesn't actually matter. What matters is that you are able to articulate the things that are of value to you and that you can define ways to measure them.

But which work is valuable and which isn't? A simple model that can help you to understand this is Dude's law,[2] created by David Hussman[*] in 2010. Dude's law states that value can be expressed as "why" over "how" (V=W/H). In other words, the more significant the outcome (why) and the less effort spent on the mechanics (how), the more valuable the piece of work will be. At the extreme case, any "why" we get for nothing has almost infinite value. Similarly, high effort for low significance has negligible value. Beware of the falsehood of high value for no effort — the critical business rule of TANSTAFL[†] applies.

It's also important to realise that there are different aspects of value. Value is in the eye of the beholder and in the context of the product. Both the why and the how will vary based on the type of value being explored at any point in time.

When you look at defining value from an outcome, you need to consider the multiple stakeholders and their perspectives. For a commercial organisation, the ultimate arbiter of value is the customer: someone who will pay real money to receive the value promised in the product or service. Customer value is not the only consideration — there is value to stakeholders and shareholders as well — and you must be able to generate that customer value sustainably and profitably.

Value could be financial return, related to organisational sustainability, meeting regulatory compliance, delivering a social benefit to the community, or almost anything else. Value can also be reduced through delay or

---

[*] Shane and David also discussed Dude's law on InfoQ's Engineering Culture Podcast. https://www.infoq.com/podcasts/david-hussman
[†] There ain't no such thing as a free lunch.

Dude's Law: Value = Why / How

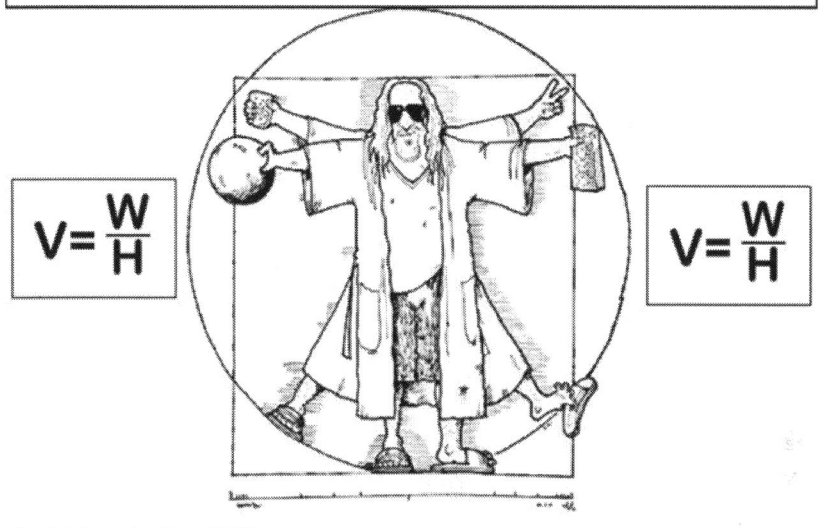

$$V = \frac{W}{H}$$

$$V = \frac{W}{H}$$

Dude's law, by David Hussman.

poor quality. Making the trade-offs about what dimension of value matters most is one of the toughest aspects of product development.

However there remains significant nuance in how value interacts with the world. Consider three aspects of the lifecycle of value creation:

1. Value degrades. This is actually the entire point of #noprojects: if you don't keep up with change, you've already failed. The value generated by any activity, once implemented, will begin to degrade. The rate of degradation depends on the context but is sadly inevitable.

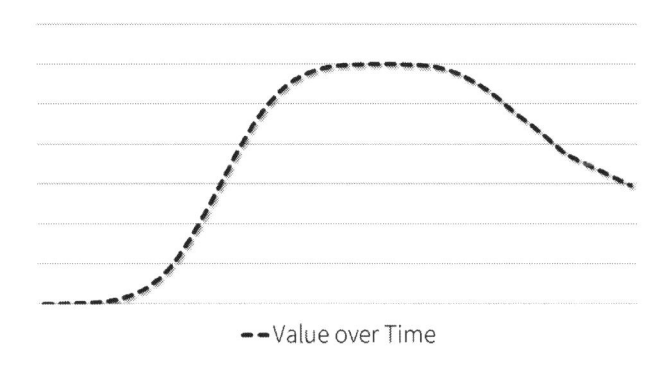

– – Value over Time

2. You don't always work on the highest-value activities first. Activities with dependencies and due dates may, of necessity, precede high-value activities.

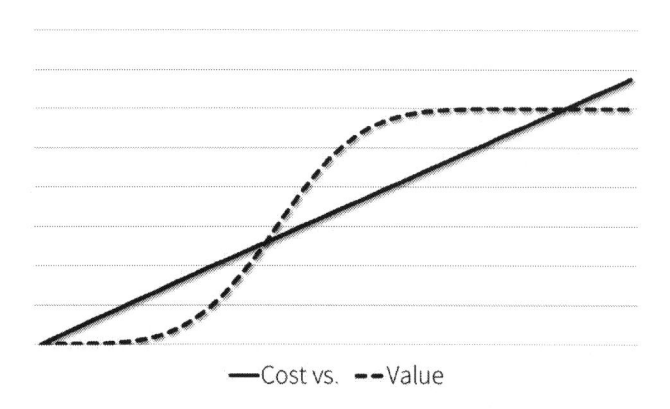

—Cost vs. --Value

3. There are local maxima. If you find that your activities aren't having the desired improvement to the outcome, you sometimes may need to reduce the overall value of the outcome temporarily in order to increase it later — e.g., removing functionality from a product in order to simplify further development. This can happen when you have reached a point of diminishing returns or if the cost of change (or innovation) has increased exponentially.

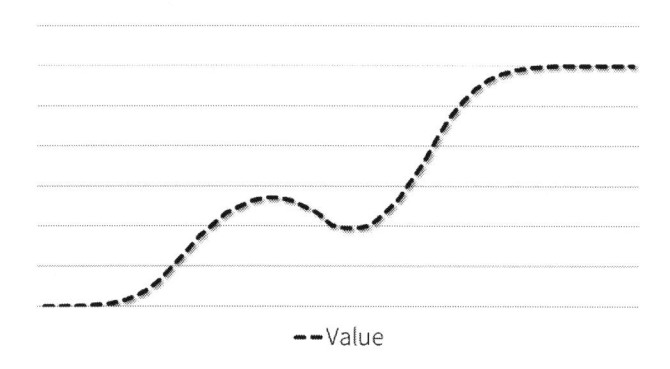

--Value

The assumed value in any activity is unproven until something is delivered that either confirms or negates the value hypothesis of the activity. Not all activities will have a positive impact on the outcomes; some will be neutral or even negative. This is why activities are meant to be small, independent, and measured in aggregate. This independence also means that technically every activity can be rolled back or undone. An important aspect of #noprojects is the need to make the cost of failure low, reducing the cycle time from the identification of a value hypothesis until that hypothesis is shown to be true or false.

Finally, always ask yourself "while I think doing X will add value, if I don't do it, so what?" Human beings are subject to confirmation bias,[3] which results in a tendency to assume that any idea we have had will be correct. This is the cause of huge amounts of wasted effort, unnecessary work, and redundant features in products. While hard to do, taking a "so what" view helps reduce this wasted effort.

Sometimes the activity being worked on is related to reducing uncertainty and risk in the work and thus has limited value on its own. Common categories of risk that may require uncertainty reducing activities include:

- **Business risk** — Should we build this thing? Is it the right thing to spend our money on?

- **Technical risk** — Can we build this thing? Do the people on the team know how to build it? Do we have the right tools, knowledge, and capabilities to build it to an acceptable standard?

- **Social risk** — Can we work together to build this thing? Are the team members able to collaborate and communicate effectively? Do they have a process for working together that is effective and enables them to correctly build the right product?

Addressing these risks might take the form of an MVP or prototype. This limits our investment (and potential return) until we have evidence that the value can in fact be realised.

In the graph below, the value curve is shallow at the beginning, indicating that the initial work was probably focused on enabling value later through mitigating the big risks early. You might consider point 1, where the curve starts to climb, as the point where the MVP demonstrates value.

—Cost vs.   --Value

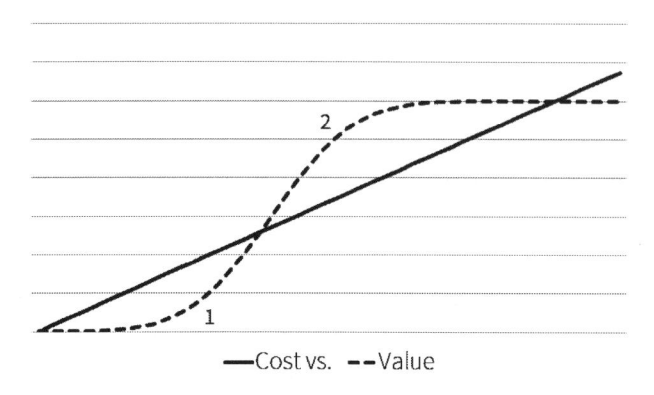

Another important element in the graph is point 2, where value begins to flatten. This is when the cost of adding the next feature or doing the next piece of work approaches or exceeds the value to be derived from it. At that point, you must ask if you should even continue the work — would the organisation be better served by stopping work on this stream of value and having the team work on something else that will deliver more value?

The difficulty with a phrase like #noprojects is that it can be perceived as a silver bullet — that getting rid of projects is a magical solution that will solve all your problems. The reality is that identifying and delivering value in knowledge-worker environments is hard to do. The traditional measures of success no longer apply.[*]

One of the most common tools for defining success has been the iron triangle of project management: on time, on budget, full scope. Many projects have defined success by this set of metrics, ignoring the two crucial dimensions of value and quality.

Jim Highsmith addressed this shift towards outcome measurement when he wrote about the new value triangle, which we have interpreted below:

---

[*] In many cases, they should not have applied before, but we can now move past them.

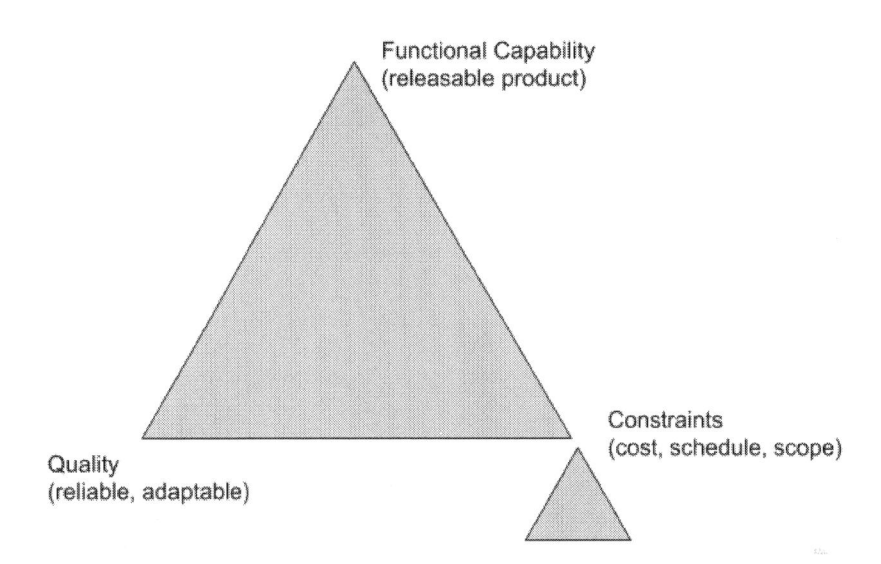

*Working with constraints —
our interpretation of Highsmith's new value triangle.*

The reality is that the three elements that were so often used to measure success are really a set of constraints. We have a certain amount of time and money to deliver the needed scope, but the primary drivers of success are functional capability (for a variety of stakeholders) and an acceptable level of quality, as these are the elements that actually make a difference to the outcomes the work achieves.

This requires defining the desired capability and quality outcomes of the work being done and identifying the constraints within which it must fit. Historically, the "triple constraint" measure of success has resulted in products that meet requirements but don't deliver value to the funding organisation. It is the relationship between these dimensions that governs what constitutes value for any given group of stakeholders.

There are certainly circumstances when it makes sense to run a project. Going back to the earlier definition of a project, project-based delivery makes sense if:

- the outputs clearly lead to clearly defined outcomes and the nature of the work is such that it really does have a defined beginning and end;
- the requirements can be defined in absolute detail and truly can be expressed in terms of the three dimensions of scope, time, and money;

- the work will be undertaken by a team who will logically disband at the end of the production activities;

- the "how" to produce the result is well understood and the nature of the work is such that it is not dependant on human creativity and individual skill (i.e., any two workers with the same skill and knowledge will produce the same result); and

- there is the ability to trade money for time, meaning that if you put more people on the task then it will be completed sooner.

An example of such a project was the team that set a world record for fastest construction of a house, whose more than 2,000 people worked together to build a house in under three hours. The planning took years and the work was defined down to the level of the individual worker on a minute-by-minute basis.[4]

Knowledge work does not fit into this category. Every initiative is different; there is no recipe to follow. While there may be some commonalities with other initiatives that have similar (or even exactly the same) requirements, the way the work is done is unique to each individual, the context in which the work is undertaken is different, and the desired outcomes will be unique to that single initiative.

Part of the idea behind #noprojects is that work usually aims to produce a product that must constantly evolve to meet the ever-changing needs of its customers. Knowledge-worker products are not stable or fixed; they are never finished, the sources of value are constantly changing, and the customer needs evolve rapidly. Shifting responsibility[*] for a product from a group of producers to a different group of maintainers requires the clarification and education of so much shared context that the maintainers might as well be the producers. In other words, the team that produces a product should be the team that supports and maintains the product in order to focus on delighting their customers and continuously increasing value.

This focus on customer delight is one of the keys to success in the modern, hyper-competitive business environment. Stephen Denning in his book *The Leader's Guide to Radical Management*[5] explains the seven principles of continuous innovation you must follow to succeed in the 21st century:

1. delighting clients,
2. self-organizing teams,

---

[*] We could just as easily call this #nohandoffs.

3. client-driven iterations,
4. delivering value to clients every iteration,
5. radical transparency,
6. continuous self-improvement, and
7. interactive communication.

These drivers of value are radically different to what it took to succeed in the 19th and 20th centuries. This is part of the reason many existing organisations find it hard to adapt and are being beaten by companies who embrace this philosophy.

Denning's first principle, of delighting clients, is the key to success: identify the people who actually use or receive benefit from your product and ensure that you make them happy. These clients are the ones whose needs come first. The project sponsor or other internal "customers" may be a source of requirements but they are never the source of value — value comes when the product in use makes a difference in someone's life.

In his book *Joy, Inc.*,[6] Richard Sheridan describes the Menlo Innovation approach to eliciting and understanding clients' needs: high-tech anthropology[7]. This approach puts front and centre the person whose life you want to change and whose behaviour you want to influence. Everything built into the product must work for the primary target persona; other stakeholders' needs matter but it is delighting that primary client that results in successful products.

With ideas from *The Leader's Guide to Radical Management* and tools like high-tech anthropology, you have ways to build delightful products, but that is not enough — you need to identify which products to build. The harsh reality is that identifying value is hard, but there are some tools that can help you compare the likely value and drivers for different initiatives, thus helping to ensure that you spend the organisation's money doing the right things. And because there will always be more opportunities than any organisation has the funding to build, these tools help you to select, from all the possible ideas, those initiatives that will be the most valuable.

The first such tool is the purpose-alignment model created by Niel Nickolaisen,[8] which is a method for aligning business decisions and process and feature designs around purpose. The purposes will generally be to either differentiate the organisation in the market or to achieve and maintain parity with the market. Those activities that do not differentiate the business in the market can often either be delivered by finding a partner to achieve differentiation or do not deserve much attention.

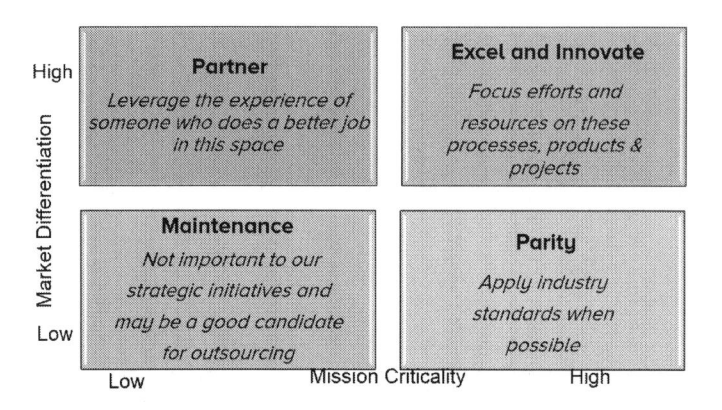

Purpose Alignment Model

	Low Mission Criticality	High Mission Criticality
High Market Differentiation	**Partner** — Leverage the experience of someone who does a better job in this space	**Excel and Innovate** — Focus efforts and resources on these processes, products & projects
Low Market Differentiation	**Maintenance** — Not important to our strategic initiatives and may be a good candidate for outsourcing	**Parity** — Apply industry standards when possible

Purpose-alignment model.

In practice, purpose alignment generates immediately usable, pragmatic decision filters that you can cascade through the organisation to improve decision making and ensure you build the right products and invest in the right things.

There are four quadrants to this model:

1. **Excel and innovate** — You need to perform differentiating activities really well; these are the things that form your competitive advantage and gain you market share. Focus on doing these better than anyone else, as they are your claim to fame. These activities link directly to strategy. Do not under-invest in these activities. Ensure that creativity and innovation focus on these activities.

2. **Parity** — Parity activities are exactly what the name says. Do them as well as the rest of the market, no better and no worse, as doing them better than the competition gives no advantage. However, they are mission-critical — they must be done well and invested in appropriately. These activities can and should be streamlined and simplified wherever possible as complexity is probably a result of over-investment, which takes opportunities and funding away from more important activities.

3. **Partner** — Some activities are not important to your core service delivery (or commercial success) but can still differentiate you in the marketplace. For those types of activities, find somebody for whom they are a core competency, and partner with them.

4. **Maintenance** — Business activities are considered maintenance if they are "neither mission critical nor market differentiating". These activities are generally intended to keep the lights on and teams should attempt to minimise the effort spent of them. These are also generally good candidates to be considered for automation, outsourcing, or simply dropping.

Having selected the level of focus that he initiative warrants, you decide amongst the next set of choices based on what aspects of the product and/or services you should build in what sequence. A tool that can help here is the Kano model.[9]

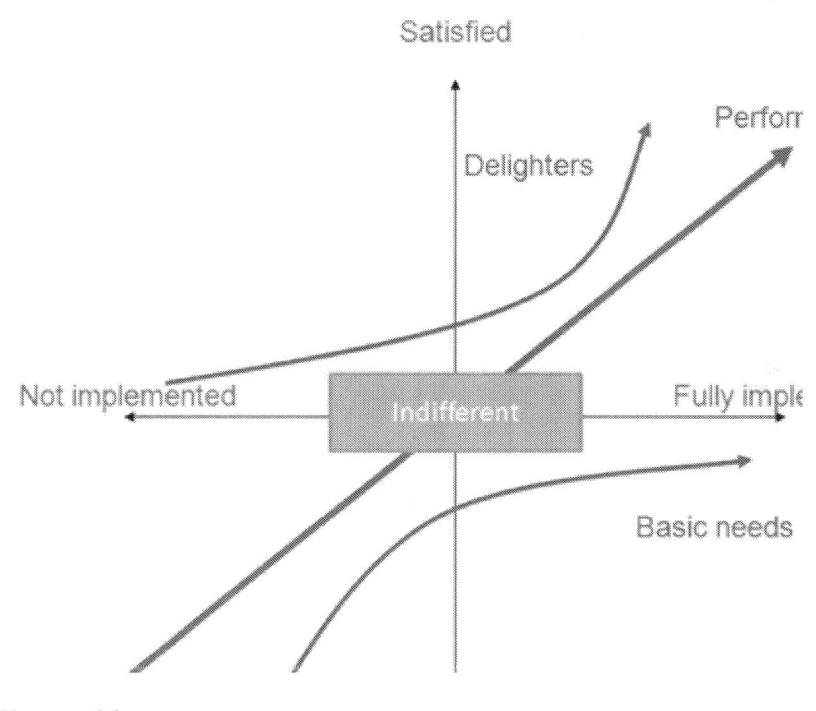

Kano model.

The purpose of the Kano model is to help you to identify those aspects and features of the product that are most important to the customer and to make better decisions about what to include and when. The Kano model focuses on differentiating product features based on your understanding of their desirability in the market.

According to the Kano model, a product or service can have three property types:

5. Basic needs — Customers expect these to be present in a product. Basic needs affect customers' satisfaction with the product or service by their absence: if they're not present, customers are dissatisfied. Even if they are present, and no other attributes are present, customers aren't particularly happy (you can see this as the bottom curve on the graph above).
6. Performance needs — These are not absolutely necessary but increase customer enjoyment and satisfaction. Higher performance in these aspects tends to result in higher satisfaction; low performance can cause dissatisfaction.
7. Delighters — These are things that customers don't even know they want but that delight them when found.

Using the Kano model

To use Kano-model analysis, follow these steps:

1. Brainstorm all of the possible features and attributes of the product or service, and everything you can do to please your customers.
2. Classify these as "basic", "performance", "delighters", and "not relevant".
3. Make sure the product or service has all appropriate "basic" attributes. If necessary, cut out "performance" attributes so that you can get these — you're going nowhere fast if the "basic" ones aren't present.

Where possible, cut out attributes that are "not relevant".

Look at the "delighters" and think how you can build some of these into the product or service. Again, if necessary, cut some "performance" attributes to afford your "delighters". Select appropriate "performance" attributes so that you can deliver a product or service at a price the customer is prepared to pay, while maintaining a good profit margin.

Continually re-evaluate the position of the features in the product and new ideas that emerge — the position of a feature in the model can change over time, moving from "delighter" to "performance" to "basic". To do this, you need good metrics.

Modern organisations thrive on metrics. They try to measure everything and use the knowledge acquired to adapt and respond. The problem is that they all too frequently measure the wrong things. By measuring things that are easy to see and record while ignoring metrics that are hard to identify and collect, organisations fail to grasp what is really happening in the ecosystem.

Easy metrics work relatively well in simple* environments. If you're manufacturing ball bearings then counting the number produced over time is important, and targeting the Six Sigma quality results (less than one defective ball bearing per million produced) makes perfect sense. Once you leave the simple domain and move into complicated and complex work environments, you need to look at different metrics to guide decisions, provide immediate feedback to the teams doing the work, and pre-empt problems before they become crises.

Some examples of metrics† that actually matter include:

- **Value as outcomes delivered, not as work done** — Rather than measuring activity (e.g., lines of code, hours spent doing something), measure the outcome of the work (e.g., new customers acquired, increased time spent viewing page, additional sales made).

- **Productivity (value/cost)** — Measuring cost and value independently won't show the real return from the effort expended. There is always a cost to deliver value.

- **Benefits realised** — Ask yourself which of the organisational goals are moved forward by this value delivery and by how much? (What is our percentage market share in a particular product type? Have we achieved market penetration in a particular geographic area? How many new patents have we had granted in a time period?)

---

* Obvious in the Cynefin model.
† Special thanks to Pat Reed for her insight in identifying these.

- **Quality** — Measure the qualities that matter for this product (e.g., a reduction in customer complaints, improved response times, or capacity metrics).*

- **Customer satisfaction and employee engagement** — Use net promoter score (NPS) to survey your customers to see how committed people are to the product. Likewise, you can use NPS with your team members to measure how engaged they are with the organisation.

- **Organisational capability and responsiveness** — How quickly does the organisation respond to customer feedback and changing market conditions?

- **Speed of learning** — What new things have you included in the product in response to customer feedback? Similarly, how frequently do new ideas appear, how quickly do you evaluate them, and how efficiently do you decide to discard or keep them?

Understanding value, both from the perspective of choosing the right "thing" to do and how to keep doing it right, gives focus and direction — in other words, "why". Now that you have, as Simon Sinek[10] famously put it, started with why, you need to look at the "what". In all but the simplest of organisations, deciding what to create falls within an actively managed portfolio of initiatives. Within a #noprojects context, this portfolio needs to be adaptive to be successful.

---

* Often referred to as "non-functional" aspects of a product.

CASE STUDY
It's never just "an IT project"
by Larry Cooper

A major Crown corporation in Canada was looking to procure and implement a learning-management system. The organisation positioned the project as an IT project: gather the requirements, procure a product through an RFP, install it, and migrate the data from the existing system. They hired me to lead both the IT and business teams.

This case study captures the story of how "an IT project" was transformed into an outcomes-driven business initiative that delivered substantially more value than planned, all within its original time and budget allocations.

I led both teams in combining business and IT frameworks, methods, and practices in a non-dogmatic manner to clarify the "why" for the project. The process of discovery enabled the business to redesign the problem to be solved in business terms, rather than in technical IT ones.

I introduced the business and IT teams to outcomes management, a modified version of the business-model canvas to define, design, and build the business services on offer, a services catalogue modelled after the ITSM space, Scrum and other agile approaches to run an agile procurement, and agile approaches to designing, developing, and deploying learning content and for business processes.

Problems

The corporation had recently decided to place staff in Canadian embassies and missions around the world. All of its existing training for its products and services were classroom-based. With the increasing geographic dispersion of its people, continued use of classroom-only training was deemed to be cost-prohibitive and would cause undue delays in the roll-out of new products and services.

The project had a fixed time of 18 months and a $2.5-million budget. The original project definition was to simply procure and implement a learning management system (LMS) in the way that most IT projects are defined in traditional settings. The IT team already had a product in mind for the LMS, which would cost $1 million.

When I arrived, I was given a copy of an RFP that a similar Crown corporation had used to procure a LMS; it was 246 pages long. The corporation had a number of Scrum coaches on site, who delivered a one-day introduction to Scrum for everyone on the cross-functional team. Scrum had not been used for a procurement project before, and the coaches indicated that it would not be a good fit. However, the executive gave the teams and me no choice: we had to use Scrum. That order, having a sample RFP for a LMS, and IT already focused on a specific product were major challenges to overcome. As well, the Learning and Development (L&D) group within HR also had little to no experience with developing learning content for online delivery.

Solution

The L&D group, along with the program-management office (PMO) within IT, felt that a cross-functional team of business and IT people, augmented with contracted workers, would be necessary. They also wanted the entire effort to use Scrum, including for the procurement of the LMS.

The IT PMO hired me to lead the cross-functional team, with reporting lines into both business and IT. The programme manager and the L&D director provided clear-the-path leadership for their respective groups. Where necessary, they were able to escalate to their respective VPs, who also strongly supported the approach.

During the first three to four months, I asked a lot of "why" questions as I introduced the team to a series of approaches to help them plan out an iterative and incremental approach to the work:

- We used an outcomes-driven approach that used back-casting to define the ultimate, intermediate, and immediate outcomes.

- The resulting outcomes map (see Figure 1) identified the required portfolio of initiatives that we would have to undertake and what each initiative would need to accomplish, as well as the order in which we would execute them.

- Each initiative was purpose-defined to deliver a specific portion of the strategic intent (i.e., the immediate, intermediate, and ultimate business outcomes to which they would contribute).

- We created a modified version of the business-model canvas called the service canvas. It helped the L&D team to capture their current services and define the new ones that would be needed (see Figure 2). The red text in Figure 2 depicts the new additions.

- We identified the required business capabilities that we would need and updated them based on the outcomes map and the service canvas.
- A technique for prioritising business value proved instrumental in saving 98.5% of the originally forecasted budget of $1 million for purchasing the LMS license. (This saved the corporation over $200,000 each year thereafter in software-maintenance costs.)
- We redeployed the $975,000 in procurement savings to the creation of the new services as well as the processes and supports necessary for creating learning content for the new LMS

I had previously implemented two other LMSs, one for a private client and the other for a public-sector client. While the first one was done without an outcomes map, the client similarly viewed it as "an IT project". I managed to get the business and IT to agree to take a business-process perspective of what had to be done, as it was a commercial-training delivery organisation that had previously been writing off 18% of their annual revenue due to bad process. Within three months, the organisation implemented the process and accounted for every penny, and there were no transactions in error. Within six months, they had an ISO certification on their processes.

The public-sector one was done using outcomes mapping from the outset. These experiences were leveraged to persuade the L&D group and the program office to give the recommended approach a try.

While the original plan had only called for the procurement and installation of the LMS along with data migration, the creation of an outcomes map identified a considerably richer and detailed set of strategic initiatives that would be necessary to realise success at a business level, as can be seen in Figure 1 and in the list of value streams under "Implementation" below. Initiatives are depicted as boxes, assumptions as triangles, and outcomes as circles. The "clouds" are used to represent value stream areas — note the overlaps.

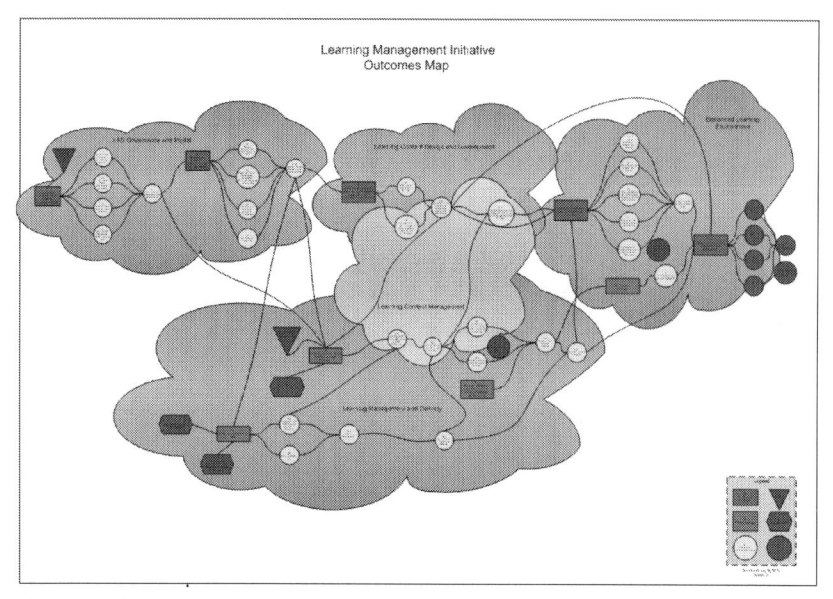

Figure 1: Outcomes map.

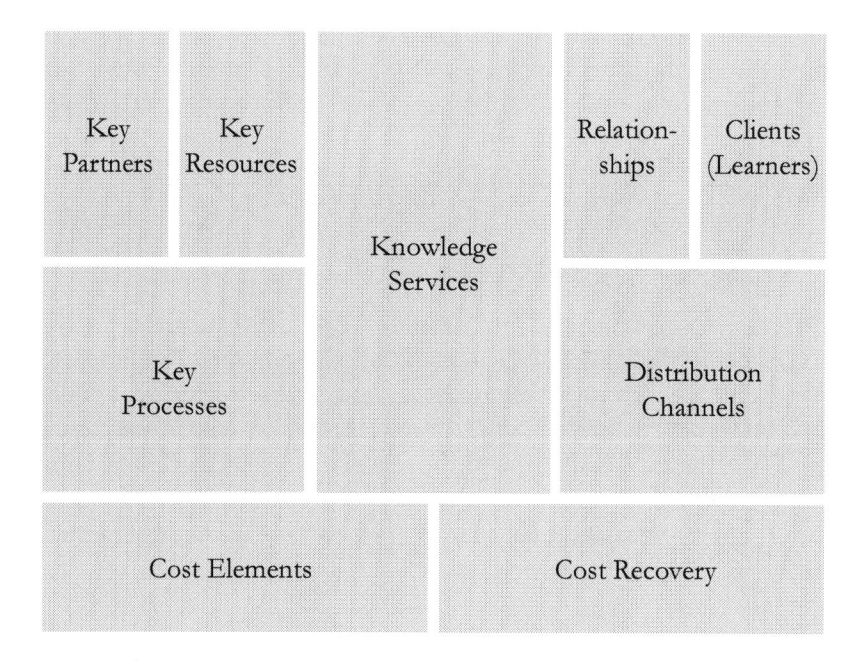

Figure 2: L&D business-services canvas.

Implementation

To achieve these outcomes, we identified five value streams along with nine purpose-defined initiatives and related immediate (secondary bullets) and intermediate (main bullets) outcomes as shown.

L&D governance value stream

- Develop and implement learning-governance model
    - » Learning-governance model is implemented.
    - » Organisational accountability for learning is defined.
    - » L&D role in talent management is defined.
    - » LOB/CoE roles/responsibilities are clear.
    - » L&D/LoB/CoE engagement model is ready for use.
- Develop and implement a learning shared-services model
    - » Learning shared-services model is ready for use.
    - » Revised measurement model is ready for use.
    - » Consistent intake, assessment, development, and delivery processes are ready for use.
    - » Performance consultant processes are standardised.
    - » L&D roles are redefined.

Learning-content design and development value stream

- Develop and implement learning-content design, development, and management processes
    - » Courseware design and development processes are managed through workflow.
    - » Learning-content design and management processes are implemented.
    - » Learning architecture is defined.
    - » Learning-content design, development, and management processes are standardized.

Learning-content management value stream

- Establish learning-content hosting in a single repository
    - » Consistent learning is achieved.
    - » Collaboration amongst learning-content developers occurs.
    - » Learning content is managed using a single repository.

- » Learning content is easier to find for reuse.
- » Learners can locate learning-content creators.

Learning management and delivery value stream
- Select and implement the LMS
    - » Learning content is dynamically delivered.
    - » Integration with required systems is achieved.
    - » LMS is implemented.
    - » LMS is installed.
- Establish relationships with external L&D service providers (learning content, knowledge management)
    - » Organisational knowledge is increased.
    - » Consistent learning is achieved.

Enhanced-learning environment value stream
- Develop and implement distributed learning channels
    - » Distributed learning channels is used.
    - » Marketing intelligence is incorporated in learning.
    - » Social networking is incorporated in learning.
    - » Forums are being used to share knowledge and capture learning needs.
    - » Structured, field-based coaching is implemented.
    - » Knowledge transfer between sector teams and business is facilitated.
- HR analytics integration
    - » HR competency decisions are supported.
- Develop and implement integrated talent management
    - » "Customer centricity" is supported.
    - » Risk reduction is achieved.
    - » Sales and revenue increases.
    - » Compliance is achieved.

The original project plan saw this as one single project. The outcomes-driven approach made visible a portfolio of nine separate business initiatives, each with specific contributions to the overall strategic intent. Note that eight of the nine initiatives would never have been done, at the least neither with the same degree of clarity around their purpose nor within the original timeline and budget, had I not introduced the teams to new-to-them business and IT frameworks, methods, and practices.

We created backlogs for each initiative and delivered them in two-week time boxes. We used VersionOne to manage the initiative backlogs. As the PMO was using MS Project Server for tracking and reporting of financials and overall delivery timelines, we agreed to only show in MS Project Server the sprints under each initiative with a comment indicating what each intended to deliver as well as a link to the VersionOne backlog. This enabled the PMO to collect the financial data they needed to report on while the project team worked in an agile way with a clear focus on business value.

We held daily stand-ups in the same place at the same time each day. We secured a team room and used it extensively throughout the 18 months of the project. We printed the outcomes map and services canvas on 36-inch-by-48-inch sheets and posted them in the common area of the office. We supplied stickies and pens so people could add comments. This approach led to numerous impromptu discussions in front of each canvas, which significantly enhanced shared understanding as well as the completeness of our vision. We would collect the stickies once a week and update both posters. We also held numerous workshops with different parts of the business across Canada to clarify our strategic intent.

To better understand what the LMS needed to do for the business, I facilitated a series of workshops over a two-month period. During each workshop, we helped the team identify required business capabilities along with more detailed statements for each capability area. When they felt they had a sufficiently complete picture of what they needed from the LMS, we had them rank each statement in each capability area on a scale as shown in Table 1.

Scale	Business Value
1	Very low
2	Low
3	Medium
4	High
5	Very high

Table 1: Business-value ranking.

Once the team ranked all statements, I then had them do pairwise comparisons of like-ranked statements, starting with the 5s. For each pairwise combination, I asked, "If you only had $1, and you could only buy one of these, which one would it be?" If they answered with one choice, the other was downgraded to the next lower number (i.e., a 4 if it had been a 5). If the response was indecisive or two items were considered equal in value, then both options maintained their current rank.

When the team evaluated and re-ranked all statements as necessary, I then asked the L&D leaders and their team members about those items ranked 1 or 2, of low or very low business value to them. Did they still want to include them, which would add much complexity to the bid responses as well as potentially skew the vendor rankings, or would they like to drop all of them?

They chose to drop the items that they had deemed to be of low or very low business value. The reduced the resulting RFP to 10 pages (from 246) and mostly explained the process we would use for evaluation. All vendors were required to submit electronic-only responses to the bid.

The evaluation team was able to complete the evaluation process in a single day. The top three vendors were invited to a boardroom demo in front of key business users. Following these sessions, we swapped the ranks of the number one and number two vendors due to vendor number two's better user experience; we had made clear in the RFP that users have to be able to use the LMS to support the required business capabilities. This meant that there was no room for bid challenges based on the process.

We also made the agile way of working part of the vendor evaluation — we wanted to make sure the vendor we chose could work the way we were. The winning vendor did.

We took only five business days to go from receipt of bid responses to selecting the winning vendor.

The overall RFP process was completed in less than six weeks leading up to vendor selection.

Challenges

The biggest challenges were with the IT support staff and the IT architecture team. The IT support staff wanted a specific product, which is where the original $1-million budget number had originated. They made several attempts throughout the project to have their preferred tool selected.

The architecture team, upon finding out that the selected product ran on Windows instead of their preferred Unix (the IT support team's product was Unix-based) engaged in a formal challenge of the procurement decision, which resulted in a two-month delay in the final contract award.

Throughout both sets of challenges, the programme manager and the L&D director remained steadfastly behind the decisions of the team. Once we overcame the IT architecture team's challenge, the IT support team dropped their challenge.

Another challenge came from the L&D team that developed the course materials. They had to move from developing classroom-only materials to developing content for online delivery. This meant:

- identifying new roles and processes relating to content design, development, and deployment;
- using a more iterative and incremental approach to content design, development, and deployment;
- having to procure and learn new content-development tools and new practices; and
- adding a content management system to the solution.

This is what led to the value streams for learning-content design and development and for learning-content management.

The final challenge came from an unlikely source. While the work was underway, another team was looking at lean process design. The approach led to a challenge for the L&D team that was developing the new processes, primarily for the learning-content design and development and learning-content management value streams. The L&D team were told they had to develop the "as is" before creating the "to be" processes and were told to do that for the developing content for online delivery — except they had never developed content for online delivery before. This created unnecessary work and tension between the teams, though we resolved it prior to going live.

Outcomes

The direct additional benefits for the organisation from the approach used included:

- clarity around what L&D did and the service commitments they would uphold for their business clients as documented in a service catalogue (no such catalogue existed previously);
- support for online and blended-learning delivery (previously, only classroom delivery was done);
- new processes for learning-content design, development, deployment, and management that were not part of the original plan;
- contributions to initiating talent management, which were also not part of the original plan;
- an agile procurement saved $975,000 in the LMS purchase and over $200,000 in annual LMS licensing; and
- the $975,000 was redeployed to deliver business value that had not been identified as part of the original project.

These benefits were achieved within the original budget and schedule, which were estimated based on only procuring and implementing a LMS along with the migration of data from the existing learning administration system.

While the defined outcomes from the outcomes map guided decision making throughout the various initiatives that we executed as part of the portfolio of work, the outcomes that would be relevant to any organization that used similar approaches include:

- Outcomes mapping (or similar maps that focus on business value) allows teams to clarify strategic intent and establish the "why" before focusing on the "what", "how", "who", "where", and "when" — you get to design the problem you want to solve without needing to know a lot of the details before you start.
- It helps teams to think of the big picture while they work in the small on purpose-defined initiatives.
- A service focus connects the "why" to the "who", which in turn provides even greater clarity on the "what", "how", "where", and "when".

- The use of maps and canvases provides big-picture visibility while enabling constant validation and adjustment throughout delivery, leading to greater shared understanding and completeness of vision.

At the end of the 18-month engagement, I was asked to deliver a series of presentations on the approaches to the programme managers, project managers, and business analysts.

PART SIX

Adaptive portfolios

Adaptability is a survival tactic for modern organisations. The lengthy planning and implementation cycles that characterised management in the 19th and 20th centuries, when budgets could be set and plans made a year or more in advance, are no longer tenable. Changes happen on a cycle of days and weeks, and organisations that can allocate people and resources to respond to these pressures turn adaptability into a competitive advantage.

Of course, every organisation is different, and this difference needs to be accounted for in the structure for and application of delivering value. How many products and services does the organisation sell and support? What are the different channels to their customers? What is the legislative ecosystem they exist in? How are they distributed? Where are people located? What constitutes value? These and many more factors mean that there truly is no "one size fits all" approach to value management and that each implementation needs to be tailored for the context of the specific organisation.

This doesn't mean that you shouldn't have strategic goals, nor does it negate the need for planning. However, it does change the approach to planning: interpreting the future as a series of horizons. Strategic goals look out a year or more, then get translated into initiatives. Each initiative will have milestones and checkpoints to ensure the work being done aligns with the organisation's goals and that scarce people and resources are being deployed in the wisest way possible. These milestones and checkpoints are not based on arbitrary tasks defined in a sequence but by incremental delivery of tangible value.

The key to portfolio thinking is a wide risk profile. Pick some sure bets that will provide a guaranteed return and take on some chancy opportunities that could win big — but consider that they could fail. When failure occurs, ensure that it happens quickly and for the lowest possible cost. A strategy of small, continuously evaluated investments is the best way to keep the risk (or blast radius) small.[1] This requires empowering teams to manage the flow of work so that it is based on discrete pieces of business value that can be delivered and evaluated on a regular cadence.

The following diagram shows the flow of work at the portfolio level.

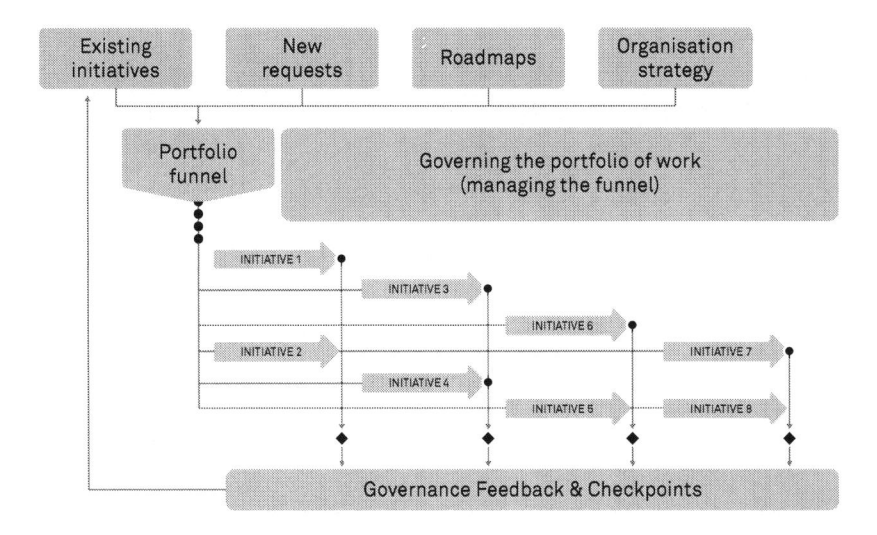

Flow of value through an adaptive portfolio.

Some initiatives will be highly experimental and should have planning cycles measured in days and weeks. Others may have more certainty in their understanding of customer needs and may have longer planning cycles, sometimes with roadmaps extending out a year or more. Even with long roadmaps, three months should be the longest planning horizon for almost any initiative as the reality is that the cascading uncertainty in longer planning cycles will likely cause massive change pressure.

All items in a portfolio have a clear lifecycle, with necessary governance checkpoints. At each checkpoint, you need to make a courageous, evidence-based decision about the next increment of investment or stopping work on this product or service — even if that means abandoning partially completed work. In other words, once sufficient value has been delivered or it has been shown that there is no value left to be extracted, it is important to be able to stop one initiative and allow the value-delivery team to work on something that is more important.

Simple, clear rules for these checkpoint decisions[*] make it practical to devolve the decision about continuing or stopping to the people doing the work wherever possible. There needs to be clear auditability of the

---

[*] We could call these "gates", but that term implies getting permission from some governing group or committee and we're explicitly advocating removing the permission-based, lack-of-trust approach that most governance models impose and replacing it with a trust-based approach that assumes that the people making the decisions are acting in the best interest of the organisation, while ensuring that the decision rationale is clear and visible — trust and verify.

decisions made and the rationale for them. This is not about getting permission to make a decision, it's empowering people to make decisions and hold themselves accountable for those decisions.

This requires careful management of the backlog of work to slice it into discrete, valuable, implementable pieces. This backlog refinement is a constant and ongoing activity that requires clearly defining what is valuable and the capacity available to deliver. Having a well-refined and well-managed backlog permits agility in delivery. Stopping work doesn't mean discarding what has been done so far, it only means that the work is sufficient for delivering an outcome for now and you can free up the capacity to focus on more valuable work. This means you may stop sooner than originally planned (if you have done enough to realise the planned value or learned that the plan was unrealistic) or later (if you learn there is more potential value to realise from continued investment) — the metric of success is not meeting an arbitrary date or even a fixed budget but rather is maximising the value to the organisation from the work done and not doing more than is needed.

The cycle in which you re-evaluate initiatives should directly relate to the planning horizon of that particular product and should take place roughly halfway through a planning cycle. If the initiative has a three-month planning horizon then this governance checkpoint should occur every six weeks.

The key is to be able to ruthlessly evaluate the value delivered by an initiative and recognise when the cost of building the next piece exceeds the value to be derived from having that piece. This means that everyone involved in the initiative needs to be willing and able to let go at any point — careers, promotions, and bonuses mustn't be linked to individual initiatives but need to be based on overall value delivered for the organisation.

Stopping work on an initiative does not mean disbanding the team; it means enabling the team to pull the next-most-important initiative from the backlog (which could be a different set of features for the current product or a completely different product) so that they are always working on the most important pieces of work in the organisational-level backlog.

An adaptive portfolio is a key characteristic of a truly learning organisation, one that listens and responds to the ever-changing voice of their customer. Peter Senge wrote, "In the long run, the only sustainable source of competitive advantage is your organisation's ability to learn faster than your competition."[2]

These ideas bring a radical shift to the traditional PMO role. This group has been responsible for ensuring the "success" of projects against the triple constraints of time, cost, and scope. Value and quality, while sometimes paid lip service, were largely ignored in the drive to meet requirements. Adherence to a defined process, audit trails,[*] and transaction logs are used, in part, to avoid blame[†] and are also key contributing factors to a manager's promotion and success.

In an adaptive portfolio environment, the PMO becomes the VMO — the value management office, responsible for maximising the value delivered to the organisation from the items in the portfolio. The VMO is empowered to make decisions about stopping and starting work on an initiative based on the changing needs of the organisation and an understanding of strategic priorities.

This is a radical shift in thinking for many organisations and PMO teams. They have to find new ways to define and measure success, new ways to evaluate what will and won't be undertaken, new ways to fund initiatives, and new ways of working. Being process police no longer[‡] adds value. Rather, the VMO takes on roles of coaches and mentors who can help teams identify the best way of working in a particular context, becoming valued partners and trusted advisors.

The organisation strategy and goals need to be clear and communicated in such a way that everyone understands what they stand for, why it matters, and who they are. This enables the formation of a decision-making framework to help to identify priorities and select from competing initiatives. One approach is to create a value model that ranks the different aspects of the organisation's operations and goals with weighting factors.

By articulating the value model, everyone in the organisation has a tool to guide decision making and ensure they align with the organisation's target outcomes. This means people can feel empowered to make good decisions without needing to escalate every question to get permission.

---

[*] "Can you send me an email with that?" is often said — the implication being "I need it in writing to cover my arse later."
[†] "I did my part correctly, so it must be someone else's fault."
[‡] We maintain that it never did.

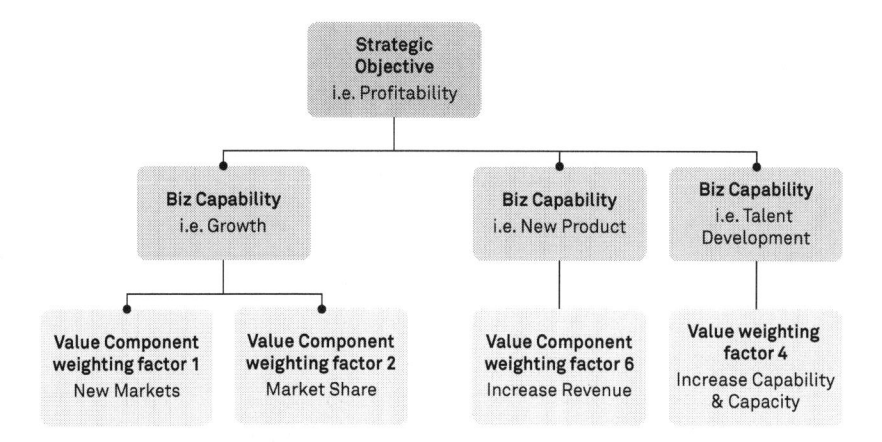

```
                    Strategic
                    Objective
                 i.e. Profitability
        ┌───────────────┼───────────────┐
   Biz Capability   Biz Capability   Biz Capability
    i.e. Growth     i.e. New Product  i.e. Talent
                                      Development
     ┌──────┴──────┐        │               │
Value Component  Value Component  Value Component  Value weighting
weighting factor 1  weighting factor 2  weighting factor 6  factor 4
  New Markets    Market Share    Increase Revenue  Increase Capability
                                                    & Capacity
```

Having identified the value elements, or value dials, it is important to weight them — how important is this factor compared to the others in achieving the strategic outcomes of the organisation? The value model communicates the relative importance of the different strategic outcomes and can be used to compare and rank different ideas by assessing which value dials the idea will move and how far — then to identify the smallest experiment that will confirm or contradict those assumptions.

The portfolio backlog is a regularly reviewed pipeline of new work and existing initiatives. Each initiative has clear, and published, metrics based on the value dials it is contributing to. Progress towards achieving the planned value is constantly assessed through built-in feedback loops and validated learning.

Each initiative is further broken down into the deliverable elements, ideally in small pieces that can be delivered independently and evaluated against measurable goals. The activity canvas is an ideal tool for identifying and managing these.

Realistically, some initiatives might need to be quite large to realise value, but effective portfolio management aims to avoid big chunks as much as possible. This does mean that the portfolio needs much more active management and ongoing refinement than has traditionally been the case — it's not "fire and forget" for a year or more at a time but is a series of carefully aimed, actively guided missiles launched in the competitive battlefield.

This backlog or pipeline contains those items currently in flight along with ideas that have passed the feasibility check and are waiting for launch.

It is important to quickly quantify the feasibility of an idea: to rapidly ascertain if the idea has wings. The goal of this step is to articulate the primary hypotheses around the idea, conducting rapid experiments to determine if there is actual demand for this product or service, aligning on the real business value, and selecting an approach to doing the work. Stopping bad ideas early is one of the most important aspects of the feasibility check.

Inflight initiatives should also be regularly checked for continued feasibility. At each checkpoint, examine the whole portfolio and make decisions about starting, stopping, and redirecting every initiative underway — has it delivered sufficient value, have we learned enough to know that we should stop and abandon this work, where should we pivot?* Will continuing to invest in this stream of work be more valuable than having the teams focus on something else?

Rank items in the portfolio against each other based on potential and actual value, cost (of delay, necessity, and compliance), risk of doing and of not doing (business and technical), available skills, and capability to deliver. You need to quantify these factors and you can use the value dials to guide your decisions.

There will be some things for which the cost of not doing the work far outweighs any savings to be made from not doing it — e.g., ignoring a compliance directive in a heavily regulated industry can result in the organisation being shut down. These types of decisions are relatively easy; others are harder and must be made based on the value hypothesis of the initiative against the value dials.

Those initiatives that pass the prioritisation test and are ready to be worked on require a roadmap of the key capabilities needed over time. The product roadmap is a time-based view of the key features and characteristics that you currently believe the product will need to deliver in order to achieve the vision. Although these will change when real customers get their hands on the product or start using the service, so be careful not to be wed to any particular feature or feature set. The roadmap typically spreads across a number of quarters and prioritises the capabilities to be delivered based around at least four factors:

---

* This is a horribly overused and misunderstood term. To pivot is to stand on one foot while changing direction, not jump to a completely new location. Abandoning one product in favour of another is not a pivot, it is choosing to discard and abandon the work already done. Pivoting leverages what has been done and takes it in a new direction.

1. Marketing needs — What key marketing messages does the product need to support in what timeframes?
2. Technology changes — What are the important technology shifts the product must be able to support over the coming months/year?
3. Market events — Are there particular external events the product should support or that need to be avoided (for example holidays and festivals)?
4. Capabilities/features identified by product management — These are based on identified needs and market feedback.

The roadmap is a picture at a point in time and is updated frequently based on the feedback from the delivery cycle.

	Q1	Q2	Q3	Q4
Marketing needs		Trade show in Jakarta		
Market events	Lunar New Year		Ramadan	Holiday sales in USA
Technology changes			Next Android version	
Capabilities/risks	Initial sales capability	Loyalty programme	Privacy legislation changing	Loyalty rewards for holiday sales
Resultant schedule	Catalogue and sales	Customer registration	Wishlist	Reward redemptions

An example of a product roadmap that looks out four quarters.

Capacity alignment is where you map the work to be done against the organisation's capability to deliver. There are two key principles that need to be in place for the most effective throughput at the team level: diverse value-delivery teams and pull-based workflow.

Diversity in thought and background is an advantage. Diverse teams consistently produce better outcomes.[3] Bring together people with different backgrounds, skillsets, attitudes, and viewpoints in an environment that encourages collaboration.

There is also a lot of evidence[4] for the value of stable teams in knowledge-worker environments. Teams who remain together for extended periods are more likely to achieve a high-performing state. They understand each other's working and communication styles; they gel and balance strengths and weaknesses and produce more value faster than temporary teams who disband and re-form frequently. This productivity improvement is also associated with higher team and individual satisfaction and stronger employee engagement — win-win in every dimension.

Any team has a limited capacity to deliver work that flows into it, and this needs to be clearly understood by all. Multitasking[5] and overloading teams are dangerous and have a significant impact on productivity, morale, and quality of work. Allowing a team to keep focus on a single stream of work and letting them manage the rate of flow based on their capacity has been shown to be the most effective way to accomplish creative knowledge work.

This means maintaining a clearly prioritised activity canvas for the team to work from, that they are able to finish one item before starting on the next, and that there are as few bottlenecks and interruptions as possible. Stopping a task in the middle to pick up something else and later coming back to the original one has a devastating impact on productivity. Gerald Weinberg examined this as far back as the 1980s and found a 20% productivity loss for every additional task a team is expected to work on simultaneously. So, if people have to switch once per day between two tasks, their available capacity for either task is no more than 40% with the 20% task-switching overhead; if they have to switch between four things then they will lose 60% of their capacity to cognitive-switching overhead and have no more than 40% available for actual work.[6]

Allowing the team to manage the rate at which they work[7] and keeping them focused on one item at a time means they produce value faster and speeds up the overall throughput of the team.

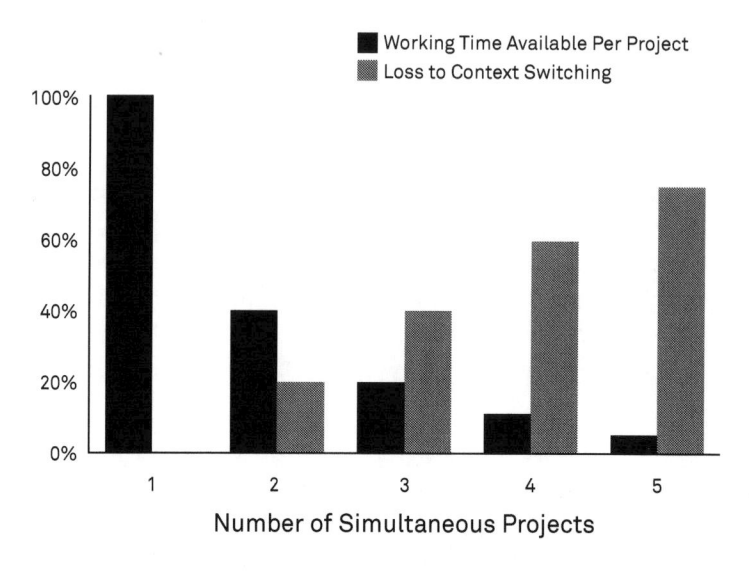

```
                ■ Working Time Available Per Project
                ▨ Loss to Context Switching
100% ┐
 80%
 60%
 40%
 20%
  0%
       1      2      3      4      5
        Number of Simultaneous Projects
```

Gerald Weinberg's productivity loss due to context switching.[6]

The whole concept of adaptive portfolio management is based on regular, truthful feedback. How is the work going? What is the quality of the delivered product? How is value being realised? What is the rate of learning? What new discoveries are becoming apparent from what has already been delivered or from the delivery process?

Teams need to report the facts, and measurements need to be built into the products to show if the outcome profile is being met. These measurements need to be based on metrics that matter rather than vanity metrics.[8] It's not how many clicks a page gets but how many new customers have registered. How many new features you have deployed is irrelevant; it's more important to measure how many people have purchased the product because of a particular feature or capability.

This requires making it safe to tell the truth and fostering a blame-free environment where learning is valued and where it is safe to fail while keeping the cost of that failure low. You need to measure the incremental success of your work while keeping the metric trends constantly visible. These metrics contribute to the prioritisation assessment every time you evaluate the portfolio.

A portfolio Kanban is a way to visualise the portfolio. Kanban is a way to depict any queue of things with a defined workflow of items that move from one state to the next. At the portfolio level, we often see two

Kanban boards: one for new ideas that need to be evaluated and assessed and the other for existing initiatives that are underway. The workflows for the two boards differ and the decision to move something from the ideas board to the initiative board is key.

Kanban is one of those tools that easy to implement and hard to master. There are some simple rules that you need to follow:

- **Visualize the work** — Focus on the whole value chain and ensure that every step is visible.
- **Limit work in progress** — You can never introduce more work than your capacity can handle.
- **Make policy explicit** — Use agreed-upon frameworks and rules.
- **Measure and manage flow** — Make it easy to identify wastes and risks.
- Define classes of service and the level of importance of each type of work item — **All items are not equal.**
- **Establish service-level agreements** — Agree on goals, which are monitored by class of service.
- **Identify improvement opportunities** — Continuously learn and adapt.

Agile Portfolio Planning Kanban Wall

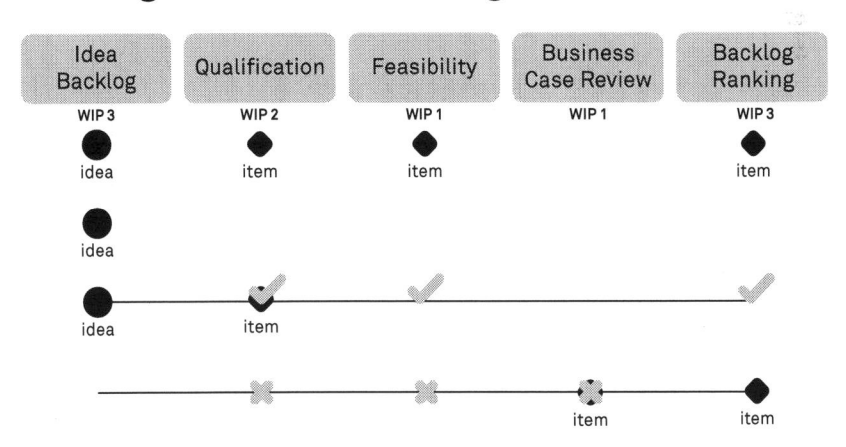

Portfolio Execution Kanban Wall

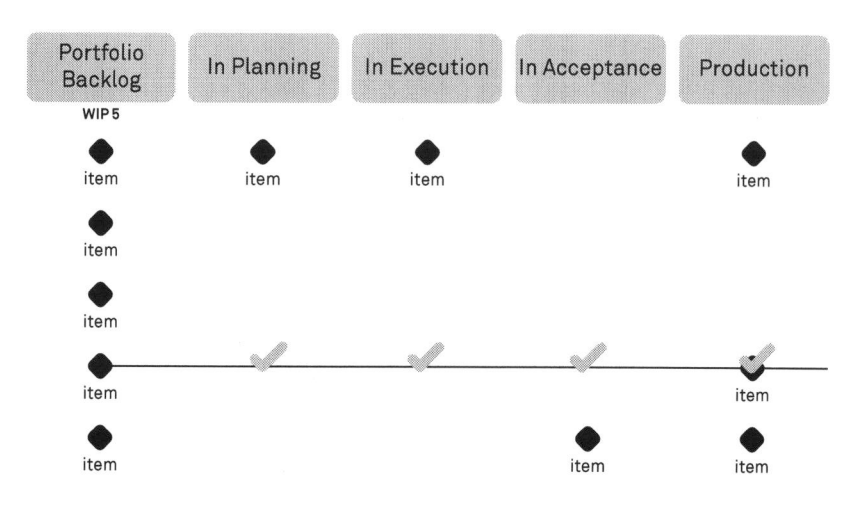

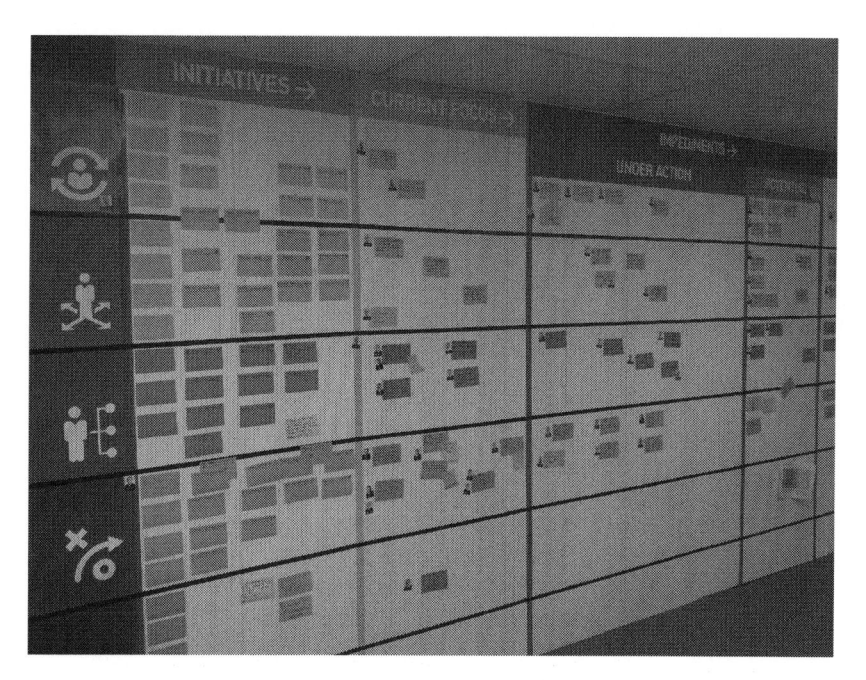

Portfolio Backlog	In Planning	In Execution	In Acceptance	Production
WIP 5				
● item	● item	● item		● item
● item				
● item				
● item	✓	✓	✓	✓ item
● item			● item	● item

New Zealand Post Group's sorting wall (an executive Kanban visualisation of all strategic initiatives in the organisation).[9]

Agile delivery is necessary but not sufficient

Agile software development was initially a reaction to the failures of predictive approaches to software engineering. It takes an empirical, feedback-led approach to building software and has some key characteristics:

- value-driven, prioritised features;
- cross-functional, empowered teams with all the skills needed to deliver working solutions;
- short cycles of work;
- close customer collaboration;
- rapid feedback; and
- constant learning and adapting for both the product and the process.

These characteristics result in better outcomes[10] at the individual product level, and agile software development has become the most prevalent[11] approach to building software today.

There is a new generation of software development teams who have never worked in a waterfall project, for whom the idea of trying to work in a predictive, sequential way from detailed requirements defined completely up front is an anathema.

Agile development uses a prioritised list of discrete items of business value to define the sequence in which items are worked on. This "backlog" is stack-ranked and work flows through the system one item at a time, with each item being completed (production ready) before the next is started. The backlog can (and should) be reprioritised frequently based on feedback from the customers and what they have learned by using the product in the wild. This reprioritisation can be as frequent as daily for highly volatile environments (production support using Kanban, for example) or less frequently for iterative delivery (e.g., in two-week sprints if Scrum is the delivery framework). By keeping the discrete items small, the flow of work through the system becomes predictable and responsive to changing customer needs.

Agile software development works at the individual team and product levels and a variety of scaling approaches[12] can apply to complex products when multiple teams must collaborate in a programme of work.

By constantly working on the next-most-important thing, teams are able to stop work on a single product at any point, and what has been done will be valuable. The Pareto principle can be applied: 80% of the value from any system almost always comes from only 20% of the features, so once the value threshold has been passed, it makes sense to stop work on that product and focus on something more important for the organisation.

The list of items in the current quarter of the roadmap is generally too big for these items to be delivered individually, and value derives from a number of features working together rather than delivering all possible options for a single feature. You have to work to turn the roadmap into a short-range backlog of discrete value items.

This requires an ongoing process of backlog refinement, which takes large chunks and slices them into a size that is deliverable in short cycles with rapid feedback. Even within a single planning cycle, however, not all items are equal and we want each delivery team to take a value-focused view of the backlog itself. The large chunks need to be broken down into user stories that the team can consume.

A backlog should not just be a list of hundreds of user stories waiting to be delivered. That approach simply results in lengthy wait times for individual stories and a large queue of work, which becomes a bottleneck and source of waste.

Once an item has been added to a backlog, it tends to take on a life of its own.[*] "Someone who matters" wants it included in the delivered product and is prepared to argue for it whenever you look at in a grooming or forward-planning session. The "someone who matters" could be a value manager, a product owner, a technical member of the team, a subject-matter expert, or any other interested party.

The normal, and generally correct, approach is for the value manager to work with the team to produce a prioritized backlog with clarity on the high-priority items and accepted uncertainty for the items that lie farther away.

---

[*] No matter how small or large it is.

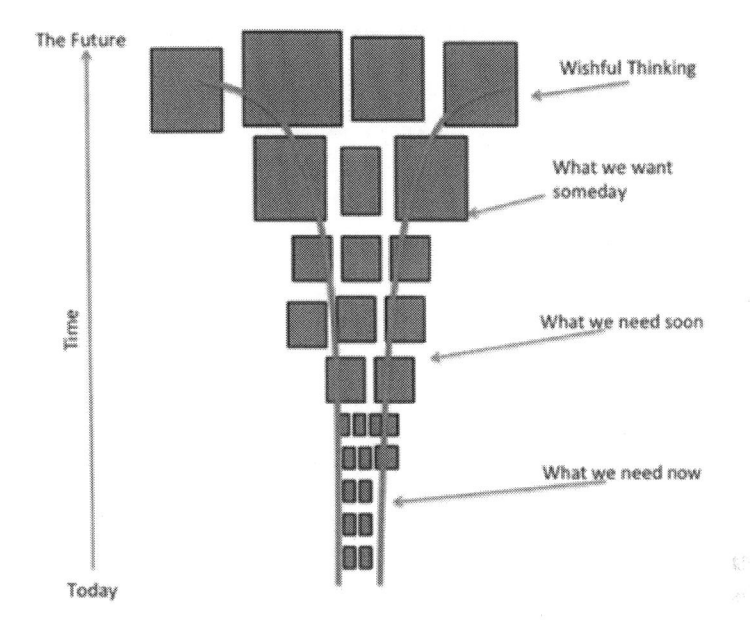

The shape of a healthy backlog.

The stories that come out of the bottom of the backlog are small enough for the team to deliver using their agile development practices. Ideally, these items should be fully implementable (per the agreed-upon definition of done) in half an iteration or less — the smaller your stories, the better your ability to predict and plan work. For those stories that are far away, however, you want to keep the level of detail coarse. The reality is that your understanding of what is needed will evolve significantly based on what happens as the product is delivered, and much of what you currently understand will turn out to be mistaken or obsolete. You must accept the VUCA nature of business needs and defer the detail until the last responsible moment.*

This continuous revision, refinement, and adaptation is a reflection of why #noprojects is so important for success in the volatile business world. Continually delivering the right work at the right time moves the organisation towards achieving the outcomes it needs to be successful.

---

* Which is quite distinct from the first irresponsible moment.

We live in a VUCA world

The world is in a state of VUCA:[13]

- **Volatility** — The rate of change is faster than we have ever experienced and is getting faster.

- **Uncertainty** — We have no clarity about future outcomes and even when we believe we know what we want to achieve, the rate of change means the goal posts move before we've had a chance to do more than take a few steps in that direction.

- **Complexity** — There are myriad factors that interact to influence the outcomes we could achieve. These interactions are often unclear until after they have happened.

- **Ambiguity** — There is haziness in almost every view of the future. We easily misinterpret events, their consequences, and their causes.

This presents a challenge for organisational planning and drives us towards a different approach. The multi-year portfolio of a stream of projects that are completed sequentially leaves us without the ability to change direction and adapt to the VUCA realities that surround us.

PART SEVEN

Delivering work

Here is the raison d'être of everything we've been talking about so far: continuously delivering the right work at the right time. In #noprojects terminology, we call these activities; "a discrete unit of work undertaken by a team to generate value in the context of a business outcome".

Unlike a project, there is no end to this work and so we cannot create a meaningful plan or schedule. There is a natural end of life to all products and services, but that is a strategic decision to be made based on the value and outcomes generated. In most cases, that is far enough into the future that attempting to predict it is pointless.

As we've seen from the success of agile delivery frameworks, you can't even predict what will be the right work to do six months from now and attempting to do so is futile in most cases. What you do know are the long-term business outcomes that you are trying to achieve and the short-term measures and targets that define success.[*] With these, you can actively, and continuously, manage the pipeline of work to achieve these outcomes.

That's where backlog management and tools like the activity canvas come in.[1] By continuously assessing, ranking,[†] and reranking potential work, teams ensure that they are working on the most valuable activity (defined as having the greatest potential impact on the business outcome) at any given point in time.

But first you need to know who is accountable for the work. There are some general principles that apply:

1. Except in the smallest of organisations, high-level outcomes will be shared amongst multiple teams, but each team should operate as independently as possible. To that end, it doesn't really matter if an individual team is accountable for a sub-outcome or a shared outcome.

2. Each team owns their own independent backlog, as explained in the previous chapter.

3. Each team is accountable for their own work, ensuring that it creates value and doesn't negatively affect another team.

---

[*] And if you don't, you weren't paying attention in the previous three chapters. :-)
[†] We want you to forget the word "priority" — it doesn't matter how important something is (everything is important to somebody). Rather, we want to know which is first, then second, then third, etc.

In general, the activities delivered by each dedicated value-delivery team (to achieve an outcome) exist on a continuum: small to large effort against low to high value. Using a visualisation tool like the activity canvas, teams have a simple way to plan the backlog. By definition, doing nothing* takes no effort and produces no value, and so sits at the bottom left.

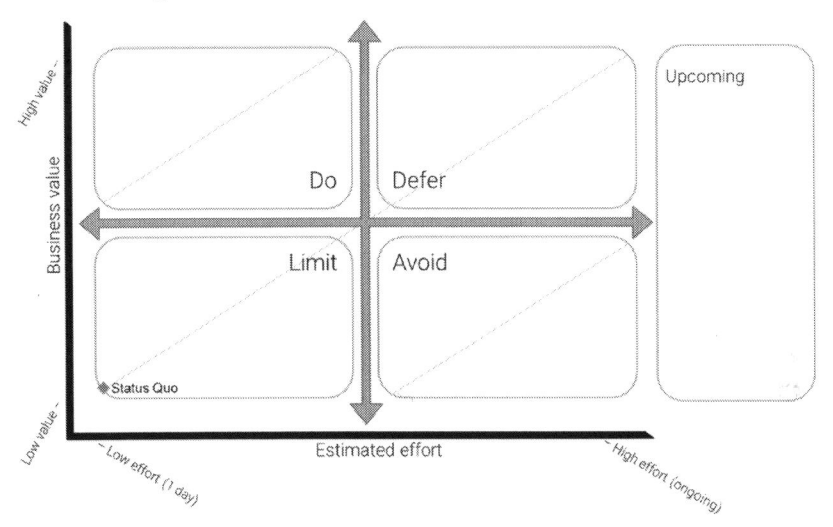

The activity canvas.

Activities in the Do quadrant are relatively easy to perform and make measurable progress towards the outcome. Those in the Defer quadrant are important but costly and need to be planned appropriately. The Limit quadrant, usually your hygiene processes, should still be undertaken but only when needed or as time permits. At the bottom right is the Avoid quadrant, and it would be rare for you to undertake any activities here.

Activities that you know are coming up but which you're not yet ready to plan can be placed beside the canvas in the Upcoming section. This allows you to keep track of anticipated work without overloading the board.

This begs the question: why would you bother adding anything to the Avoid quadrant? In short, it's because this is an active management tool and as you continuously reassess each activity, activities may change quadrants (e.g., from Avoid to Do) as circumstances change.

---

* Keeping the status quo.

#NOPROJECTS: A CULTURE OF CONTINUOUS VALUE

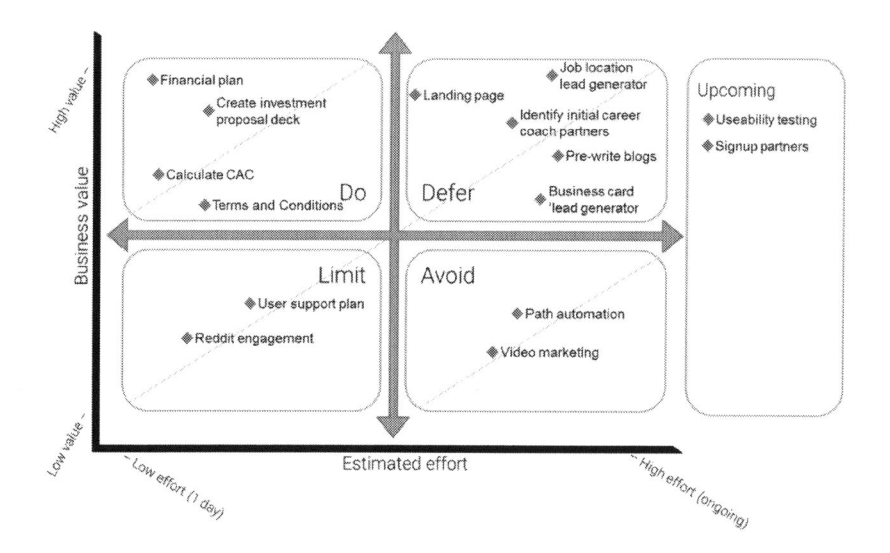

A sample activity canvas for a startup business.

An additional benefit of the activity canvas is that it encourages teams to reduce the overall size of their work, which naturally leads to smaller batch sizes, faster deployment, and evidence-based ROI decisions.

Here's a reminder about value: in most cases, value is highly subjective and hard to quantify. This is expected and is part of the risk of doing business. After all, if you could accurately predict the return on every investment, being in the market would be a lot safer. When ranking activities on the value axis, compare each activity against its peers — is A more or less valuable than B (in the context of the outcome)? If you can quantify an activity, (e.g., revenue generated, cost of delay, user requests, etc.) then definitely do so, but don't rely on this in all cases.

But remember: always measure the outcome.

Having a clear understanding of value will also help to ameliorate the impulsive knee-jerk reaction that occurs when a something changes on the canvas.* The activity canvas is not a queue, where the first, latest, or loudest voice wins. No matter the order in which you add activities to the canvas, the next activity to be taken off will always be the top-left-most activity.

Now, because each activity is small, the direct impact on the outcome may also be small or even unmeasurable. But what you are interested in is the

---

* And it will change. Often.

cumulative impact of all activities to the outcome. Therefore, the team should at regular intervals measure their progress against the outcome's baseline measure(s), although the form of measurement will depend on the outcome and how it is quantified. The organisation can then use these measurements to make informed decisions about future investment and strategic directions. Depending on the result, the team may set a new target within the outcome profile or even change the outcome entirely — which will, of course, also result in changing the backlog.

Each activity on the canvas should be independent. That is, it could be removed from the canvas with no impact to any other activity. Obviously, this is not always possible, but it should be a key consideration when designing activities. If you're finding that none of your activities are independent, try creating canvases at multiple levels, such as one canvas for master activities and separate canvases for sub-activities within each master activity.

INVEST

When defining an activity, it should meet the INVEST characteristics, as defined by Bill Wake:[2]

- **Independent** — Each activity should be as self-contained as possible, with minimal dependencies on any other activity. This allows for easy reordering or removal as circumstances change.

- **Negotiable** — An activity can change at any time up to the point work commences.

- **Valuable** — Each activity should deliver tangible and (in aggregate) measurable value towards the outcome.

- **Estimable** — The definition of each activity is such that the team can estimate it.

- **Small** — The estimate and delivery of an activity should take place within a few days to a few weeks.

- **Testable** — Each activity should have appropriate quality control, so that what is delivered can be assessed against the intent.

By defining independent activities, each of which delivers value within the context of the outcome, a pattern emerges. Focus changes from prioritisation (high, medium, low) to order (1, 2, 3, 4, 5...). That is, you no longer care what activities are high priority, you care about which is first. A natural side effect of this is the overall reduction of work in progress, which in turn increases the throughput and productivity of your teams.

Based on this, you can draw a path between your activities, starting from the first to the final activity. All else being equal, the standard path should look something like this:

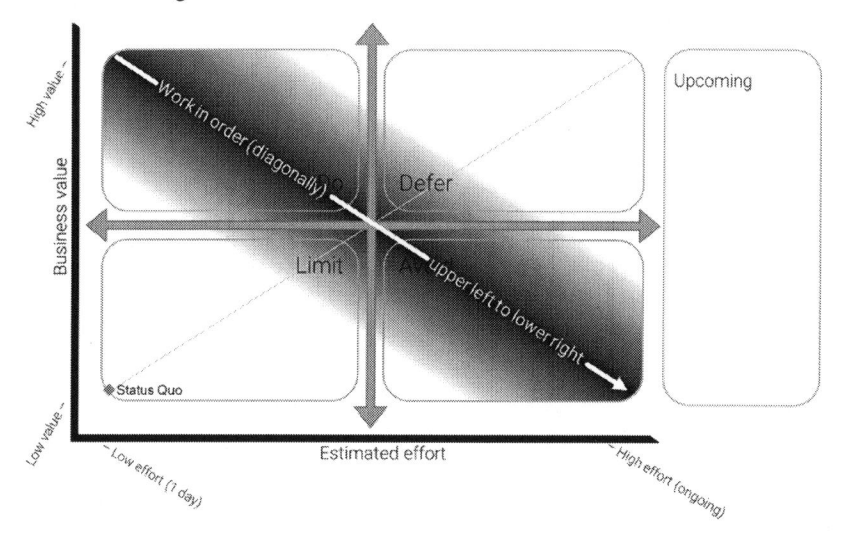

The order of work on an activity canvas.

But what if all else isn't equal? Activities with fixed due dates or dependent activities will naturally impact the order of work. Dependent activities should be rare if you're following the principle of independence. Where they exist, you can redraw the path based on the new order. This will also help you identify and streamline common dependencies.

Activities with a fixed due date are anomalous but expected. These may jump to the head of the queue regardless of which quadrant they are in — although activities in the Avoid quadrant should still be avoided when possible.

DELIVERING WORK

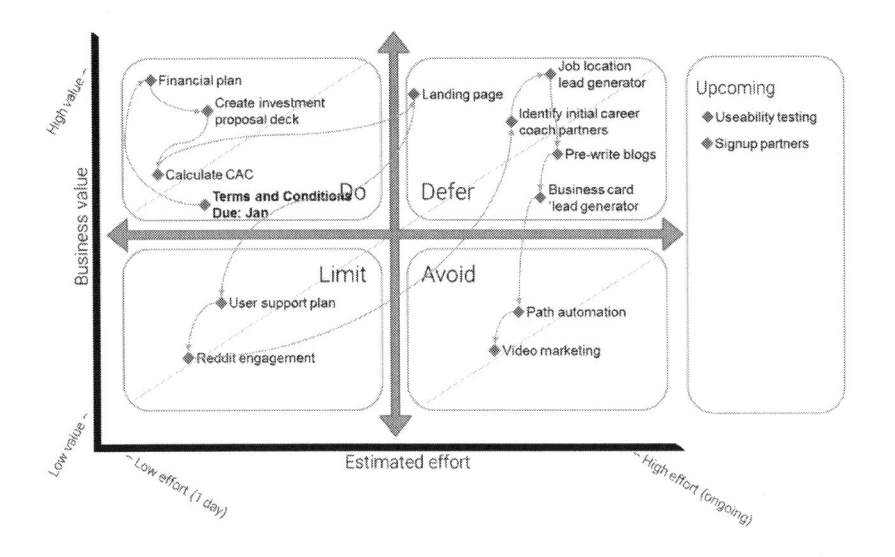

(Quadrant chart: Business value (low→high) vs Estimated effort (low effort 1 day → high effort ongoing). Quadrants labeled Do, Defer, Limit, Avoid, with an Upcoming box.)

- **Do** (high value, low effort): Financial plan; Create investment proposal deck; Calculate CAC; Terms and Conditions Due: Jan
- **Defer** (high value, high effort): Landing page; Job location lead generator; Identify initial career coach partners; Pre-write blogs; Business card lead generator
- **Upcoming**: Useability testing; Signup partners
- **Limit** (low value, low effort): User support plan; Reddit engagement
- **Avoid** (low value, high effort): Path automation; Video marketing

The order of work for a startup business.

You want to look at the Defer items on a regular basis to see if you can break them down into smaller pieces, which could then move into the Do quadrant. By slicing activities this way, you are often able to deliver the core value earlier and leave higher-risk or complex parts for later or discard them completely.

There is another benefit to this approach: by actively managing your activities, you can identify structural problems with your value-delivery team. When activities appear on the board (especially in the Do and Defer quadrants) faster than they are being completed, it is likely that you do not have the right number or mix of skills. Use this opportunity to run a retrospective to analyse the root cause of the issues and either increase your team's capacity or identify a different approach.

This brings us to the final point. It doesn't matter what the work is. Nothing that we've discussed here is specific to software development (or accounting or manufacturing, for that matter). As long as there is a level of unpredictability in the outcome, the teams are trusted to make operational decisions, and value can be continuously created, a #noprojects approach works.

CASE STUDY
Using the #noprojects paradigm
by Max Roy

I was involved in building and delivering mission-critical applications for a semi-governmental organisation that provided emergency-management services in Australia. This ICT department was relatively new, hence was not saddled with bureaucratic decision gates and governance procedures. They identified four main applications as the core deliverables that would support the emergency services provided by the field personnel. A select team of individuals was formed consisting of:

- the ICT manager, who also functioned as the de facto ScrumMaster;
- an in-house developer;
- an in-house database administrator;
- a business subject-matter expert (SME); and
- vendor personnel as needed.

There was no project plan with detailed work assignments. There was no assigned project manager, though the organisation does have a sort of project management office that oversees external communications and liaisons. We did no financial estimates or cost/benefit analyses before commencing each mission-critical application, hence we had no approvals to obtain from a peak body such as an estimates committee before commencing the work or when making changes to the system functionality.

The application architecture consisted of four major applications that exchanged data with mission-critical external organisations, such as State Emergency Services (SES), and published information to the community. The applications had to be distributed across a dedicated WAN network so that operational units throughout the state could enter and update their transactional data.

The initial estimate, provided by an external consultancy, for the end-to-end implementation of the four applications was about AU$37 million. The estimate was the result of a month-long engagement with the consultancy organisation. During this engagement, the consultants met with the key stakeholders and IT personnel to gain familiarity with the organisation's operations and culture.

The IT manager decided to set aside the consultancy's findings and commence building the applications with the team defined in the list above. Happily, he did not have to negotiate a bureaucratic decision-making process through levels of senior management before commencing. He adopted a #noprojects paradigm in that there were:

- no extensive boilerplate documentation, such as solution architecture or detailed system design, on the lines of Prince2 or other project-management methodology, prior to building the applications;

- no project schedule with defined start and end dates and consequential penalty clauses for not meeting them; and

- no annual budget allocations or approvals from the financial controller.

The team used an agile approach in:

- consulting with the embedded business SME to list the functionality and features of each application, prioritising the features to work on based on business value;

- building the features, both database design and coding, in short iterations (one to two weeks);

- having the business SME approve the feature implementation at the end of each iteration cycle;

- dynamically changing the system design in response to feedback;

- holding retrospectives at the end of each sprint to determine lessons learned and what worked best; and

- releasing to production when a logical piece of work had been completed (e.g., when the functionality for resource type "vehicle" was done in the resource management system, the business SME tested it, and once approved, it was released into production for the end users.)

As mentioned, there were no project deadlines or penalties for not meeting them.

The end users for these applications were:

- about 1,200 brigade personnel who entered incidents, resources (vehicles, equipment, etc.), and their response compliance times;

- district, regional and head-office personnel who monitored and sometimes updated the information and generated extracts for external reporting and compliance purposes; and

- analysts who interacted with the applications to report on statistics, trends, and other analysis.

We built the four applications and released them to operations within 18 months at a cost of around AU$3 million — less than one tenth the cost estimated by the consultancy! The production releases had no major issues and they continue to operate successfully, providing value to the business.

Throughout the course of application development, the team adopted a continuous-delivery paradigm of functionality and features. We built prototypes of feature sets in the test environment for the business SME. Once we reached consensus on the prototype, we commenced the actual database changes and coding. We followed this with integration tests with other impacted applications before production releases.

Excluding changes in vendor personnel, the in-house team has remained intact and cohesive, with an average engagement of more than eight years in the organisation. Although such lengths of engagement within the same group may be exceptional for the IT industry, there is a definite advantage in having a close-knit team delivering continuous value. In contrast, when there are frequent changes of personnel within teams, new members must acquire domain knowledge and build new working relationships. This invariably leads to delays and loss in productivity as team members adjust to each other and obtain knowledge and skills.

The team acquired deep domain knowledge as well as close, trusted working relationships with business SMEs. This included the technical personnel, who understood the business processes involved because of their long association with the organisation. Furthermore, the ICT manager insisted that everyone share their knowledge, especially regarding the underlying use cases and business rules. Thus, the team were able to respond quickly to any new or changed business requirements. The team continues to function this way, with high levels of cohesion, information sharing, and client satisfaction.

Finally, a key feature of this approach was the lack of any arbitrary financial overrule on the scope or functionality of application delivery. There was nothing the team needed to submit to a project estimates committee or similar organisational authority to obtain approval before commencing any new application functionality; neither were we saddled with any obligatory outsourcing contracts. The business outcomes were evaluated via feedback obtained from the end users. The ICT manager with the business SME, under direction of the product owner, negotiated for the funding required for the next body of work, which then commenced immediately.

PART EIGHT

Continuous culture

Why now? What is it about the current market and economy that makes #noprojects a viable approach? The simple answer is that customers now expect this. We call this "continuous culture". The market expects continuous change and improvement in the majority of our products and services. Everything you see around you is continuously changing and improving,[*] in all aspects of your life.

The half-lives of phones, advertising, and the age of companies[1] are all evolving — as is even the way you live. As we mentioned earlier, people change jobs almost as often as they change phones (every 4.2 years according to the US Department of Labour).[2]

What does this mean for organisations? It's more than just understanding continuous change, it's understanding continuously continuous. It means that companies can no longer rely on the corporate five-year plan, or even a short project plan, to remain accurate.[†] Let's examine that for a moment.

Strategic planning is the process by which an organisation defines the projects, initiatives, and actions (the plan) that will achieve their corporate vision or mission. It is traditionally time consuming, with lots of data collection and meetings of executives. Once the plan is complete, it is presented as a fait accompli[‡] to the rest of the organisation for implementation. However, ask any executive[§] and they'll admit that this process doesn't work — there are few real innovations and the plan itself is usually out of date before it begins.

An agile or continuous organisation wants to move away from the traditional, static planning process towards a dynamic and agile strategy that can adapt as the market changes. We might also call this a "learning organisation",[3] one that uses an "inspect and adapt" feedback cycle to continuously create and refine their corporate strategy.

---

[*] At the very least, things are changing. Hopefully, they are improving at least most of the time.
[†] Not that it ever was.
[‡] An "accomplished fact" or thing that has been done — everything sounds better in French.
[§] Over beer.

Running a strategic planning workshop in an agile organisation

Agile strategic planning starts in the same place as in a traditional organisation: with the vision and business outcomes for the organisation. And while the vision may change to meet market demand, it usually changes very slowly. Executives come together to agree on, and align to, the vision and outcomes (and the part of it that they are accountable for). But here's where it diverges: rather than spend months creating and agreeing to the plan, the executives agree on "how" to plan. They agree on an approach that they and their teams will use to:

- incrementally create and refine the specific initiatives that will work towards the vision;
- embed continuous improvement into the process;
- inspect and measure the impact that current activities are having on the vision; and
- allocate funding to the initiatives — and, if they know the expected value (to the organisation) of the work and continue to inspect and adapt, they don't need to know what it will be spent on ahead of time.

This process will generate some of the business outcomes that are run using all the techniques mentioned in the last few chapters. Therefore, this should be an inclusive process; mature agile organisations bring the entire company (or representatives, for massive companies) into the process. This doesn't mean sending out surveys and asking for feedback — this is to get the teams deeply involved in the planning and decision-making process itself. In some cases, the teams will decide on the vision rather than the CEO and board.

Because accountability for outcomes sits with the teams themselves, it means that strategic decisions are generally made at the lowest level, by the people who are doing the work and have the most information. The organisation forms dedicated teams around the strategic outcomes and interface points with the rest of the organisation. Don't treat these as stretch goals. This is the critical work needed to realise the corporate vision — and if the vision isn't important, don't waste everyone's time.

Finally, the feedback cycle: because you're dealing with strategic initiatives, you usually don't have the same instant validation that you would with a product. However, you still need constant feedback — look for a combination of lagging and leading indicators that represent success (e.g., staff attrition or sales). However, be alert for and ignore vanity metrics — those that if improved would lead to no meaningful benefit to the organisation (e.g., increasing Facebook likes or team velocity).

At the product level, continuous culture emerges in strategy, marketing, and design. Successful companies directly use market feedback in their product development cycles. When listening to the customer, the traditional approach of planning a project up front for the next one to two years is no longer appropriate. Product development and design cycles are linked directly to the market and the associated feedback loop. With the right data insights, governance, and empowered teams, this feedback and development cycle can be as short as a single day.

What does this mean for projects? It means that planning a temporary endeavour with the assumption of a stable market between project start and completion is dangerous. Remember that projects generally only concern themselves with delivering the agreed-upon work, not the business benefits. Even agile projects, which release frequently, assume that the product agreed upon in the business case is the right product. As Peter F. Drucker[4] famously wrote, "There is surely nothing quite so useless as doing with great efficiency what should not be done at all."

Continuous strategy, design, and marketing approaches, with an active market-feedback loop, can completely change the assumptions behind a project business case and sometimes can even invalidate the business case. Without this continuous culture, the feedback loop in traditional projects is generally too slow to react, which is why so many projects fail to deliver the expected business results.

By building teams around business outcomes while listening to market demand and end-user feedback, #noprojects organisations are able to continuously produce the right product for the market.

Even supporting functions such as people operations,* finance, and legal benefit from the continuous culture. It's no longer good enough

---

*   Please stop calling this function "human resources". People are not resources to be consumed in the delivery of a product, they are the primary source of value and to be agile and deliver a product in a continuous way, you also need to have all of the supporting structures* aligned. With apologies to Eliyahu Goldratt, we often talk about Evan's theory of agile constraints: "An organisation can only be as agile as its least agile division!"

Goldratt's original theory of constraints[5] states that there is a constraining factor in any process and, more importantly, that there will always be a constraining factor. The theory of agile constraints states that there will always be a constraint to business agility in an organisation. Twenty years ago, that was IT. That was your software team. And that's why it was logical for Agile, capital-A Agile as in "Agile Manifesto", to emerge in that domain. Today the constraint to agility isn't IT, but rather is likely to be the PMO, finance, or legal department.

#noprojects represents work as a continuous and stable flow so it's logical to extend that across the organisation. Take a software organisation as an example. You have user or business demand on one side and the production environment on the other. Somewhere along this flow is the limiting constraint. Maybe it's taking too long for developers to deliver products. So, you introduce Scrum.

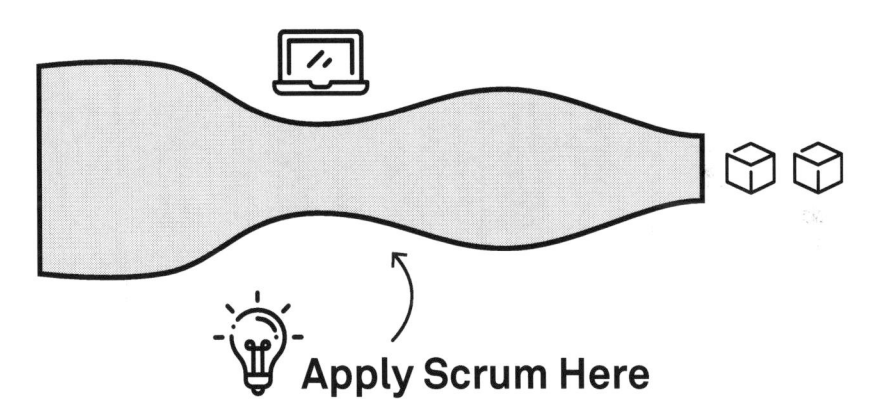

Apply Scrum Here

That opens up the flow in your development teams. Great. Except that Scrum hasn't been as effective as you'd hoped. Development is still taking too long.† Now, there's a new constraint in the system, perhaps the deployment environment. So, you bring in DevOps. Great — that opens up the flow further.

---

   innovation in our organisations.
* Or at least as many as possible.
† The sad fact is that many organisations stop here because "Well, Scrum didn't work."

Apply DevOps Here

But now, there's a new constraint. You need a wider view. You need to bring in business agility. Where's the next constraint? Maybe it's finance, your budgeting process. You have an 18-month budgeting process that limits the development cycle that can deploy every day. Fix that. Then it's HR or the PMO... — wash, rinse, repeat.

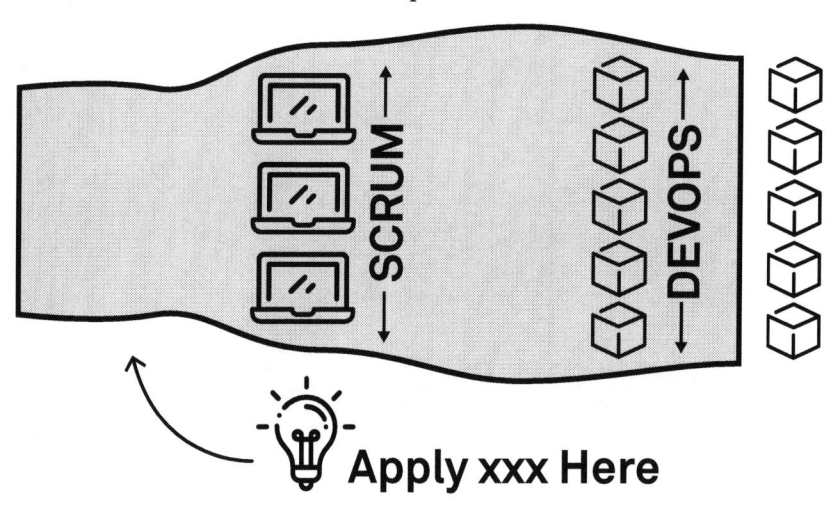

Apply xxx Here

In today's economy, these are the areas that are constraining the agility of an organisation. In many ways, this is the definition of business agility: taking the mindset of agility and the practice of agile and applying them across the organisation. But it goes beyond that. It goes into the very culture and structure of the organisation. Is the organisation designed in such a way to be competitive in an ambiguous and unpredictable market?

These are not easy problems to solve. It's not just a matter of asking finance and HR to adopt Scrum or Kanban.* There may be significant cultural and experience barriers to the adoption of the new approach. These are teams who are accustomed to their current ways of working because they have always worked that way — and in many cases quite successfully. If you want to introduce agility to these divisions, you need to communicate that this isn't about fixing a problem. You're fundamentally changing the way the organisation operates in the market. To put it another way, you are improving the outcomes for the entire organisation, not just a single division.

The point is that there is always a constraint to organisational agility, which in turn limits the ability to adapt to an unpredictable and ambiguous market.

Ultimately this leads to the concept of an agile business. A continuous business. One that is designed around flow or the continuous creation of value. Continuous culture means that an organisation is itself continuous, that the company maps to the market and the way the market thinks and reacts, rather than the traditionally assuming a predictable and unambiguous environment and creating one-year or five-year plans in that false context. That's not to say that continuous organisations don't have goals. Goals are in fact critical for success. And throughout this book, you should have seen the importance of defining clear outcomes for any engagement. The difference is that you don't prescribe in advance *how* you expect to achieve this — you allow this to emerge in response to immediate context. A continuous business means designing a team, division, or organisation around continuous culture.

This culminates in a process of continuous learning, the ability to identify new opportunities, market trends, customer demands, and internally new ways of working. But this is not some "lessons learned" workshop.† This is about using the feedback loops to apply that learning continuously. Part of your daily process is to look at ways you can improve the work being done. The market changes continuously, so if you don't continuously observe and experiment, then you're not in a position to learn from it.

---

* We don't think that's ever worked, even for software teams.

† Or as we like to call them, "lessons observed" workshops. We usually don't actually learn from them. For most organisations, the "lessoned learned" repository is a write-only system. No one ever reads it afterwards.

This is a proactive stance. Adaptive, learning, agile organisations are constantly looking for ways to improve by actively seeking feedback early and often, either through formal retrospectives or by continuously experimenting, inspecting, and adapting in the market. The goal is to maximise the value they deliver to customers and stakeholders while creating an environment of joy in work.

Continuous-learning organisations see work as experiments, as hypotheses to be tested[*] as quickly as possible. One way of achieving this is to frame each activity as a hypothesis to be tested rather than as a requirement to be met. The following is hypothesis-driven delivery[6] as extended by Pat Reed:

1. If we <do this>,
2. we believe <this percentage of targeted customers>
3. will <experience this benefit>
4. and <respond with this behaviour>.
5. This hypothesis will have succeeded when <we can measure this result>.
6. Otherwise, <next hypothesis to test or pivot>.

There is a technical aspect to continuous culture. #noprojects works best when you have systems in place to streamline the continuous change process in agile software delivery (technical agility), DevOps, continuous and automated testing, continuous integration, continuous delivery, and continuous deployment. There is a famous example in the technology industry — that Amazon deploys to production every 11.6 seconds.[7] Your specific environment might not need that frequency of deployment, but the shorter the delivery cycle, the shorter the feedback loop, and the sooner you can apply what you've learned.

We should add that this doesn't just apply to IT and software development. Obviously, DevOps is primarily a software-development practice. But the principles apply regardless of domain. Reduce the feedback loop.

The sad fact is that these technologies are nothing new. Continuous integration has been around for nearly 20 years and automated testing for even longer. It is fairly well established that organisations who adopt these technologies significantly reduce their deployment and testing costs. And we mean significantly — the *2016 State of DevOps Report*[8] had this to say:

---

[*] And failed.

> *High-performing organizations are decisively outperforming their lower-performing peers in terms of throughput. High performers deploy 200 times more frequently than low performers, with 2,555 times faster lead times. They also continue to significantly outperform low performers, with 24 times faster recovery times and three times lower change failure rates.*

A clear example comes from Telstra, the largest Australian telecommunications provider, who realised a saving of nearly $600,000 per deployment and a five-fold increase in the number of test cases run within 12 months of adopting CI and automated testing.[9]

Continuous deployment is the newest and logical progression of this; the ability to automatically deploy incremental change to the market (the production environment) has been around for a while. Fundamentally, it is a design and development technique used to automate and improve the process of software delivery. Consisting of a variety of technical practices (supported by tools) such as automated testing, continuous integration, and continuous delivery, continuous deployment allows value-delivery teams to rapidly and easily package and deploy changes to test, staging,* and production environments. This is usually coupled with A/B testing of the individual change to validate specific characteristics and identify those that are most commercially viable. Along with automated rollback, this speeds up the deployment of features and bug fixes to customers while reducing risk and overhead.

In continuous deployment, a change can be deployed when (and only when) it has passed automated testing and can be independently rolled back. If this concept is new to you, we recommend you read *Continuous Delivery* by Jez Humble and David Farley.[10]

Automated functional testing, automated regression testing, and continuous integration become absolutely essential to create confidence that the developed change is defect free. By using test-automation software, you can control the execution of tests and automatically validate the results against predicted outputs. Test-automation software can undertake thousands of regression tests in seconds and help to ensure that each individual change has not introduced defects or unexpected behaviours elsewhere

---

* Some organisations have gone so far as to no longer have testing and staging environments, reducing their need to maintain and support these platforms and freeing up as much as 30% of their IT funding. See https://www.infoq.com/podcasts/Michael-Bryzek-testing-in-production for an example of how one company has achieved this.

in the product. Note, however, that the cost of developing an automated test base for existing products without any previous automation can be significant and you will need to determine the cost/benefit ratio product by product.

The adoption of test-driven-development (TDD) techniques, the practice of writing your test cases before undertaking work, will also ensure that there is a link between good design and testing. DevOps is implicit in the design of value-delivery teams: cross-functional and multidisciplinary teams that own all the work to deliver a business outcome. This ensures traceability of a change from development to production. In fact, it would be more appropriate to describe this as BizDevOps — a continuous flow of value starting in the business rather than in IT delivery, which implements business ideas.

As a guideline, organisations and teams need to consider four elements in their design and planning:

1. **The architecture** — The architecture needs to be modular and allow for incremental deployment from the very beginning. Monolithic designs and applications do not fit this approach. That doesn't mean that monolithic or legacy applications require traditional projects, but they will miss out on some of the benefits of this continuous culture.

2. **The feedback loop** — There's no point in delivering continuously if you cannot take advantage of lessons as early as possible. You must build feedback mechanisms, both manual and automatic, into the product. These may include feature requests from users, defect feedback, feature usage, click rates, or time spent.

3. **A rollback mechanism** — If there is no human interaction with the deployment to production then there must be a significant level of confidence in the work that is being done. This not only means that a high percentage of code must be covered by automated tests, but also that the environment needs the ability to roll back any individual change at almost any point, without impacting any other feature.

4. **Safe to fail** — Organisations need to make it safe to execute a rollback without penalty to the developer. We've seen some organisations introduce failure KPIs that demand that all employees (from the CEO down) demonstrate failure at least once per year in order to

receive their bonus. The argument is that if they do not demonstrate failure, they are either hiding or not taking enough risks.

So far, all our examples have focused on software development but these approaches have been successfully applied in other domains as well. A good example is the advent of real-time marketing, which Wikipedia defines as "marketing performed 'on the fly' to determine an appropriate or optimal approach to a particular customer at a particular time and place".[11] This approach requires technology support and an adaptive mindset — just like DevOps and continuous delivery.

#noprojects is a cultural and behavioural shift caused by the emergence of the continuous culture more than it is a process or technical change. However, as in all cultural changes, the status quo will always make last-ditch attempts to remain relevant. Nowhere is this more evident than in the emergence of shadow projects.[12] A shadow project is a pattern that emerges in #noprojects or continuous-change environments where teams and divisions mimic a project structure in all but name.

We often find that these patterns emerge in organisations that do not transform the supporting processes and governance structures. For example:

- changes continue to go through a release approval board before promotion to production,
- the organisation commits to the solution defined in the business case and is unwilling to adjust even when evidence suggests that they should,
- approval is required to spend previously allocated funds, or
- there is no clear mechanism to collect or analyse the measures defined for each outcome or value-delivery team.

To identify a shadow project in your organisation, it is important to understand the characteristics of a project. Of most relevance to this is the temporary, constrained, and siloed nature of projects.

By definition, a project is a temporary structure to deliver a specific change or series of changes. This is fundamentally opposed to the principle of #noprojects, which promotes a continuous-change model that derives value from the ongoing development of new capability. A shadow project emerges when a team is formed solely to produce a single output[*] or is regularly diverted to different outcomes. This is compounded if the team is dispersed and potentially re-formed (or a different team created) to re-address the same output/outcome at a later date.

Don't mistake this for the natural end of a business experiment that doesn't produce the expected results. Similarly, don't mistake this for the natural end of life of an outcome that occurs when the value-versus-effort ratio goes negative. These are the legitimate end points.

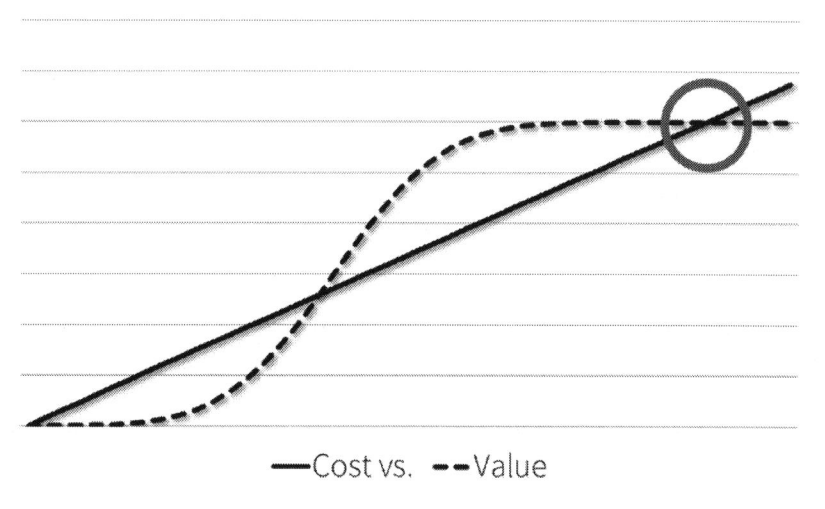

—Cost vs. --Value

The natural end of a product (maximum ROI reached).

Projects thrive in highly constrained environments, but this doesn't mean that constraints are bad. Constraints are critically important for business, doubly so in #noprojects. There are two reasons for this. First, innovation only occurs where there are constraints to overcome. Second, constraints[†] ensure that teams respect other teams and external requirements. However, shadow projects can form where there are *artificial* constraints imposed on a team — usually in the form of fixed time, fixed cost, or fixed scope. If your customer asks for a specific product or a predefined set of activities in a specific timeframe — that is a project.

Keep in mind that while individual activities can have a deadline, there is a fundamental difference between these constraints and a fixed scope or fixed goal.

---

[*] Which may be phrased as an outcome.
[†] These are the working principles described in the "Outcomes over outputs" chapter.

The siloed nature of traditional organisations* encourages detailed upfront project planning to minimise the impact of the handover between teams. And because a project is a temporary structure, the line management of the project team usually differs from the management of the project. This can lead to multiple approvals, functional handovers, and inefficient matrix structures.

A shadow project occurs when there are shadow, or parallel, approval processes between managers or functional areas. #noprojects requires only a single point of accountability, whether structured as a value-delivery team or functionality hierarchy, for all delivered activities. In other words, the most-senior line manager of the team and the specific outcome sponsor should be the same person.

The failure of organisations that do not embrace this continuous culture is self-evident. You just need to look at Chapter 2 to see examples of the failures that occur when companies do not continuously learn. Customer and market expectations are higher than ever and without this ability to learn, organisations struggle to compete. The five-year plan is long gone.

The worst part for traditional organisations is that this continuous culture is already here. To survive the next 10 years, you need to be able to react and learn quickly.

---

* Where multiple teams are accountable for their part in the process.

PART NINE

Value-delivery teams

If you accept that work should be defined by business outcomes rather than projects, then you need a new way of thinking about your organisation. Your organisation will obviously be working on multiple outcomes simultaneously and each of these will be assigned to one or more teams as required. In turn, each team needs to be accountable for planning and delivering the ongoing activities required to achieve the outcome assigned to them.*

However, projects have been so pervasive over the last century that even our organisational structures have been designed around them. In most organisations, people report in a functional silo (e.g., finance, HR, sales, or IT) and potentially also in an associated matrix function. This is perfect for forming, disbanding, and re-forming temporary teams to work on projects as needed but becomes ineffective when confronted with outcome-based work.

But before we dive into a team, let's start a little bigger. Let's look at the context in which your organisation operates....

In his book, Reinventing Organisations,[1] Frederic Laloux classified organisations within five distinct modes of operation: impulsive (red), conformist (amber), achievement (orange), pluralistic (green), and evolutionary (teal). We should note that the classification technically starts at reactive (infrared) and magic (magenta), although these classifications predate organisational structures and are generally used for pre-agrarian societies.

Impulsive, or red, organisations are the most authoritarian. They are defined by a singular, dominant leader: the alpha wolf, if you will. This leader directs staff through the direct expression of power and fear with little or no subtlety or finesse. However, this authority is fragile, and leaders tend to surround themselves with trusted parties, often family members. While this type of organisation can be particularly effective in hostile environments, they tend to quickly break down under their own impulsive nature. Thankfully, there are very few examples of impulsive/red organisations today and these are mostly limited to organised crime and militias.

Conformist, or amber, organisations use what we would define as "command and control". They are able to plan for the short, medium, and long terms, creating scalable organisational structures. They primarily operate in stable environments where they can directly extrapolate past experience to future performance. However, they are fragile in their own way;

---

* Without conflicting with other teams obviously.

when circumstances change, conformist/amber organisations find it hard to adapt. This tends to lead to organisations that strive for market dominance and monopoly.

Structurally, conformist/amber organisations adopt highly rigid hierarchical models[*] with formal reporting lines from manager to subordinate, cascading down the organisation. Control is no longer driven directly by the leader but from position in the hierarchy, which supports the creation of much larger organisations that can operate across multiple geographies. This structure also incubates a siloed "us versus them" mentality between multiple divisions as well as with external organisations (be they clients or competitors). Modern examples of conformist/amber organisations are churches, militaries, and most government agencies.

Achievement, or orange, organisations are the dominant form of company in the world today and owe their success to their ability to innovate, delegate accountability, and increase available talent by operating as a meritocracy. These organisations move away from "command and control" towards a "predict and control" model. While still strongly hierarchical, achievement/orange organisations introduce the matrix structure: a semi-independent team that cuts across silos in order to deliver a project. In theory, these matrix structures operate under "management by objective" and receive the authority and accountability to execute on their objectives. It is this form of management that gives rise to KPIs, annual budgets, balanced scorecards, and performance incentives (bonuses).

The design of an achievement/orange organisation is often undermined by many of the issues that plague conformist/amber organisations. Management by objective is compromised by the inability of some leaders to release sufficient decision-making control to their teams. And the "us versus them" mentality is compounded by the addition of competing projects (as well as competing functional areas), which further impedes collaboration.[†]

Pluralistic, or green, organisations embrace the unpredictability and complexity that emerges in complex systems such as organisations and the markets they operate in. The premise is that success and failure aren't binary options. Unlike in conformist/amber and achievement/orange top-down decision making,[‡] pluralistic/green organisations empower teams

---

[*] Pyramids.
[†] A good example of that is the competitive annual budget cycle — especially when bonuses are at stake.
[‡] Even if the decision is pushed to lower levels.

for bottom-up and consensus-driven decision making where team members are trusted to make the right decision because they are the closest to the client or customer. Alignment between teams comes about through common, meaningful values and principles that are adopted and followed across all levels of the organisation.

You can see pluralistic/green organisations emerge in many social organisations and non-profits, and more for-profit organisations are adopting these models as well (e.g., Southwest Airlines and Ben & Jerry's). The difficulty involved in gaining consensus amongst groups of individuals has meant that pluralistic/green organisations have historically struggled to find an organisational structure that works and scales. The co-operative structure is probably the closest we have. The concept of servant leadership is pluralistic/green organisations' most well-known contribution to the overall organisational landscape. These organisations retain a hierarchical structure, but this is turned on its head[*] with the leadership at the bottom supporting the rest of the organisation rather than controlling it.

Evolutionary, or teal, organisations are an emerging class of businesses. There are very few notable evolutionary/teal organisations right now, but the concepts and business models are starting to become understood. Core to these new organisations is the understanding of the company as a complex system, or even ecosystem, of interconnected yet discrete entities — be they individuals, teams, business units, or products — with their own directions and purposes. Self-management[†] becomes a critical factor; one of our favourite quotes from Laloux's book explains this perfectly. This passage describes Buurtzorg, an evolutionary/teal healthcare organisation in the Netherlands: "The vertical power transmission of traditional pyramidal organizations is taken off its hinges: the teams of nurses aren't simply empowered by their hierarchy; they are truly powerful because there is no hierarchy that has decision-making power over them."

Its emerging nature means that there is no common structure for evolutionary/teal organisations at this time. Nevertheless, in our experience, the prominent hierarchy model that has served conformist/amber, achievement/orange, and pluralistic/green organisations seems to have reached the limit of its usefulness.[‡] A dynamic network model seems to be more appropriate.

---

[*] Literally.
[†] Rather than empowerment.
[‡] We'd argue that this started with the emergence of the matrix structure.

Laloux is clear about the limitations and biases that emerge from classification. In no case is an organisation entirely achievement/orange or pluralistic/green. Different individuals, teams, and business units may operate at different classifications depending on the context. Even a single team may operate at different levels at different times. When an organisation is called pluralistic/green, it merely means that this is the dominant paradigm within which the organisation and its leaders operate.

What does all this have to do with #noprojects? Understanding how your organisation approaches work is critical to adopting #noprojects-based models. Organisations that are predominantly impulsive/red, conformist/amber, or, to a lesser extent, achievement/orange are going to struggle to adopt this style of work. Once we move away from temporary teams, team permanence becomes a necessity and so dedicated, stable teams are critical to success.

We call these "value-delivery teams".

Because value-delivery teams are accountable to deliver a specific outcome rather than an output, a new team structure emerges that by necessity integrates the skills from multiple functional areas. These stable, cross-functional teams benefit the organisation by improving coordination, simplifying communication, and sharing expertise to solve problems. This approach significantly reduces many of the overheads in traditional project structures as many of the coordination, monitoring, and reporting activities are no longer required.

And so, unlike a team formed in a matrix organisation, value-delivery teams need to be stable, need to report to a single line manager, and need to be structurally aligned to parent outcomes.* In fact, the entire point of #noprojects is that these value-delivery teams will own the changes that add value to the target outcome. Collectively, the team is accountable for the outcome — although, depending on the style of organisation, this may be expressed through a team leader. It is the team leader (or team facilitator[2] for teal teams) who also takes on the responsibility for the few traditional project-management activities that remain: stakeholder engagement, expectations management, risk identification, and so on.

Whether multiple value-delivery teams collaborate on a single business outcome (and outcome profile) or focus on independent outcomes, they all share a single purpose.† This alignment to purpose helps to ensure that

---

* Rather than functional areas.
† "Act in your company's best interest" is a good place to start.

teams do not succumb to competing with each other. Limited resources, financial constraints, and customer pressure will always put a strain on teams, and without strong alignment this tension can express itself as an internal "us versus them" mentality.

So, if you're a project manager reading this, don't fear this change to your role. Many of your project-management skills remain valuable for organisations — it's just the "temporary project" aspect that fundamentally changes.

Value-delivery teams also require a clear line of sight to the customer or product owner (in the context of agile delivery). In many value-delivery teams, the customer is embedded within the team and treated as a team member. In environments where the consumers or users are distinct from the customer, they tend not to be team members. However, it is important that the team regularly engage with them (or a subset of them, like a focus group) to validate that the work that is being produced creates value. That's what the "value" in "value-delivery team" means.

The specific structure of each value-delivery team is unique, and ideally evolves over time with guidance by the team itself. However, regardless of the structure, certain archetypes are necessary for effective teams: the facilitator, the analyst, the customer, the enabler, the architect, the builder, the communicator, and the tester. Note that these are capabilities, not people. There may be multiple roles per archetype and an individual team member may play one or more roles depending on the context.

Facilitator

Guides and enables the team to collaborate, achieve consensus, work at a sustainable pace, and meet compliance and process commitments in order to operate at peak effectiveness without sacrificing quality or craftsmanship. A servant leader who is also responsible for removing impediments, leading team meetings, and other common social practices.

Experience & Seniority: Any, but must have respect of the team

Example Roles: Agile coach, ScrumMaster, project manager

Metaphor: The nervous system

Analyst

Brings domain knowledge and works closely with users and stakeholders to understand and define their needs.

Experience & Seniority: Experienced

Example Roles: Product owner, business analyst, SME

Metaphor: The eyes and ears

Customer

Owns the final product and ultimately is responsible for the value generated and final outcome.

Experience & Seniority: Highly experienced

Example Roles: Customer, product owner, product manager

Metaphor: The spirit

Enabler

Responsible for any supporting activity that enables the rest of the team to operate at peak efficiency.

Experience & Seniority: Any

Example Roles: ScrumMaster, executive assistant, accountant

Metaphor: The heart

Architect

Designs the most appropriate solution to the context while factoring in working principles, the wider ecosystem, and any other constraint.

Experience & Seniority: Experienced

Example Roles: Software architect, modeller, UX designer, service designer

Metaphor: The head

Builder

Anybody who directly creates a piece of the product.

Experience & Seniority: Any

Example Roles: Software developer, database developer, engineer, operations, UX/UI, process analyst

Metaphor: The hands

Communicator

Clearly, succinctly, and continuously shares details relating to the adoption of the team's work.

Experience & Seniority: Any

Example Roles: Change manager, OCM, technical writer, marketer

Metaphor: The mouth

Tester

Ensures that the product is appropriate to the context or of appropriate quality and that it achieves a measure of value towards the outcome.

Experience & Seniority: Any

Example Roles: Tester, QA, business analyst

Metaphor: The immune system

While there may be a team leader or manager, each value-delivery team is expected to operate as a single, collaborative unit. No one can succeed unless the entire team succeeds. For that reason, there should be no individual KPIs, performance measures, or bonuses — those exist at the level of the team. And the only people who can judge underperforming individuals are their peers.

Don't expect that just because you form a value-delivery team and assign them an outcome, they'll immediately perform. There is a well-understood process of team formation, the Tuckman model,[3] which shows that teams must move through multiple stages before they can become highly effective. These are:

1. **Forming** — The team is new and individual members tend to act independently. They are focused on finding their place in the team and how that aligns to the team objectives.
2. **Storming** — The team is learning to work together and the natural tensions and conflicts between members emerge. Some[*] teams skip this stage.[†]
3. **Norming** — The team has stabilised as a cooperative and collaborative unit with a common goal. There may be disagreements, but the (formal or informal) social contract amongst team members provides a mechanism to manage these.
4. **Performing** — The team is now highly motivated and knowledgeable. Team members are focused on the outcome and, even if working independently, operate as a team.

This team formation takes time — in our experience, it takes at least six months for a team to settle into a performing mode and it may revert to previous states as circumstances change.

This is another reason that stable teams are so important and why organisations should avoid short-term project teams. When project teams hand over to a separate "business as usual" (BAU) team and disband at the end of a project, there is a net loss for the organisation[4] in terms of both the effort involved to form a team and the technical and domain knowledge that the team has acquired. This is compounded when a project team is made up of contractors or vendor representatives, which leads to additional costs for organisations to transfer knowledge to BAU staff. And, of course, there is significant lead time when the organisation starts the inevitable version 2 or upgrade project and needs to either find the old team members or train a new project team. This can be avoided with dedicated value-delivery teams.

#noprojects is as much a cultural change as it is a process change. As such, leaders will need to support their value-delivery teams in identifying the natural rhythm or cadence of the work they do. After all, it is the value-delivery team itself, not a manager, who are fundamentally accountable for managing the continuous flow of change and the asso-

---

[*] Lucky.
[†] And some unlucky teams never get out of this stage.

ciated real-time planning of activities. And this is true at both the macro (outcome) and micro (activity) level.

At the macro level, the cadence of work is managed through the team backlog. The sizing of the activities, the planning and delivery cycle, and the feedback loops all inform the overall cadence of the team.

Depending on the context of the team, this backlog may be the equivalent of an agile product backlog or it may contain activities from multiple products. The value-delivery team (which includes the product owner if it is an agile delivery team) is solely accountable for the content, prioritisation, and delivery of that backlog. The intention is that each item in this backlog will create value towards the success of the associated business outcome. At the organisation level, the measure of this outcome provides the governance necessary to ensure that the value-delivery team is working on the correct activities.

An anti-pattern that we see all too often is when a single value-delivery team is simultaneously working towards multiple outcomes (or for multiple clients) and switching between them frequently. This usually is a response to the question of how to manage team workload and show progress to clients when working on more than one project.* This misses the point. Team structure and organisational design should be such that focus is possible. And stop saying that you need to multitask. All that means is that you don't know how to say no, plan your work, or define clear and independent outcomes.

Multitasking like this can nurture negative behaviours in everyone. From a team perspective, it's going to be hard to keep momentum on your work. From a client perspective, neither client is going to get the focus and productivity they expect and thus will not be happy. And from a management perspective, it's difficult to measure productivity and value. In short, everything you work on will take longer than it should.

When a single value-delivery team must support multiple clients,† the team must have a single, managed, and prioritised backlog (and activity canvas) for all their work while using a continuous-delivery model. The team can then always work on the next most important task, regardless of what it is or who it is for. This also helps to answer the question of "when

---

* There's that word again. :-)
† Or outcomes.

will X be done?" By analysing metrics for lead time* and cycle time,† it is a simple matter of extrapolating how long X will take.

At the micro level, the team will have a cadence in their daily work, and leaders need to enable that. Nowhere is this more evident than in the way you plan your day. Managers typically schedule their work in hour or half-hour blocks, whereas staff tasked with large-scale work will typically schedule their work in half-day blocks. Paul Graham defines this brilliantly:[5]

> *There are two types of schedule, which I'll call the manager's schedule and the maker's schedule. The manager's schedule is for bosses. It's embodied in the traditional appointment book, with each day cut into one-hour intervals. You can block off several hours for a single task if you need to, but by default you change what you're doing every hour.*
>
> ...
>
> *But there's another way of using time that's common among people who make things, like programmers and writers. They generally prefer to use time in units of half a day at least. You can't write or program well in units of an hour. That's barely enough time to get started.*

So, an agile leader not only lets "makers" schedule their own workday but is subservient to their schedule. Should an hour-long meeting be needed, an agile leader should work around the makers' schedule. This is one of the hallmarks of an empowered employee, one who has the authority to manage their own schedule rather than bend to the whim of their manager's schedule.

We've implemented this with a few of our previous clients. Meetings, as requested by management, can only be scheduled between 9 and 11 a.m. Beyond this, the schedule for each team and each team member is at their sole discretion. This has increased both the productivity and morale of the team.

So, what is the role of a manager in #noprojects? In many ways, it is the very distinction between leadership and management. Assuming you've not gone full teal and have self-managing teams, the leader of a value-delivery team (or #noprojects organisation) is one who understands how to support and delegate. And we don't mean delegating actions‡ but

---

* Lead time is the time it takes for an activity to go from the initial request to done.
† Cycle time is the time it takes for an activity to go from start to done.
‡ "I need you to put a presentation together by Friday."

rather delegating ownership and outcomes.* If we focus on hiring good†
people, we can leave the choice and implementation of the relevant actions to them and trust that they will act in the best interest of the organisation and customer. This means that:

- Instead of "I need a presentation on X," say "we need to make our clients aware of the new products."
- Instead of "I need you to sell this car," say "we need to increase sales by 10% this quarter."
- Instead of "I need you to upgrade Microsoft Office to 2025," say "we need to maintain all systems and ensure they are up to date".

To understand the kind of leader you are, take a moment to consider your management style. W. Edwards Deming[6] put forward two types of mistake that you as a leader can make when dealing with variation in outcomes:

1. interfering or tampering when everything is normal or within tolerance (common causes), which is generally indicative of micromanagement, and
2. failure to intervene when a process is out of control (special causes), which is generally indicative of absenteeism.

As a leader, you need to find the middle ground between these two extremes.

Micromanagers tend to be highly reactive to minor, expected, or manageable issues without giving their teams the authority to resolve them internally. If a process is under control and within allowed tolerances, team members should have the authority to deliver without management intervention. This assumes a robust monitoring and reporting process to identify when assistance becomes required. This brings us to the other extreme, an absentee manager. A manager is absent, even while physically in the office, if they do not engage with their teams to help to remove impediments and blockers. Without a leader to eliminate external and, sadly, sometimes internal impediments, it becomes nearly impossible to meet any outcome.

---

* "We need to make our clients aware of the new products."
† These are people who we can trust to do the job that we ask of them. And if you can't trust them to do a good job, you have a bigger problem.

These are the attributes of a bad manager, but what attributes make a successful leader? While that could be an entire book in itself,[*] we would condense them into 10 core attributes:112

1. You can validate the pros and cons of a decision in an uncertain or ambiguous context to take advantage of change.

2. You have excellent facilitation, communication, and social skills (e.g., engaging, presenting, negotiating, resolving, and persuading) to build relationships with customers and colleagues while reducing misunderstanding and conflict. A quick wit and good sense of humour help with this.

3. You are creative and can develop or recognise new responses to problems in order to improve outcomes for your customers and reduce costs for your business. Creative leaders also tend to attract talented teams.

4. You have strength of character when dealing with stress and keep emotions out of professional interactions and decision making to build a professional environment where individuals are comfortable.

5. You are aware of and leverage your strengths and weaknesses and how they apply to your role. Teams respond well to self-confidence but not to a large ego.

6. You are self-motivated, with effective time management skills, and take accountability for organisational outcomes (visualising the short, medium and long-term outcomes while adapting to changing circumstances).

7. You have the appropriate professional and technical knowledge needed to engage with your colleagues and customers. You do not need to know enough to do their job, but enough to understand their work.

8. You understand the value of delegation, getting things done through other people, in order to improve overall productivity and promote personal development. You trust your teams and colleagues and do not fear losing control.

9. You lead your team with honesty, fairness, and integrity to create an environment where mistakes are seen as learning opportunities. You

---

[*] And several have already been written.

are willing to listen to and seek input from colleagues and you are honest about performance without being offensive or personal.

10. You are aware of the organisational strategy and your role within it so that organisational outcomes (not just team outcomes) are factored into decisions.

You may notice that nothing we've mentioned here requires a leader to be in a position of authority. In other words, a leader doesn't have to be a boss. Before we finish this chapter, let us distinguish the two different forms of authority:

1. Institutional authority — Your authority (or right to lead) is instilled by virtue of the position you hold in the organisation.

2. Personal authority — Your authority (or right to lead) is instilled by those around you.

Obviously, a strong leader (in the boss definition) should have both, but anyone in the team can, and should, have personal authority. In general, an individual's personal authority is strongly aligned to how much you trust their competence and sharing a commonality of purpose. If team members can build trust and commonality of purpose, you have a team that is set up for success.

CASE STUDY
Haier elevation
by Doug Kirkpatrick

This case depicts a global manufacturing giant grappling with the challenge of unlocking the innovative and entrepreneurial spirit of its employees worldwide and linking them so tightly to its end users that it creates zero distance between employee and customer, driving superior levels of responsiveness and customer loyalty.

Problem

Haier entered the Internet Age with a bureaucratic, hierarchical company full of middle managers, hampering innovation and business agility. Its connectivity to external stakeholders, particularly customers, was less than optimal. Many employees lacked the skills to innovate and adapt to an environment of continuous change. Haier's CEO, Zhang Ruimin, had always been a visionary advocate of adaptation and improvement. His challenge was how to infuse that vision into a global manufacturing concern.

Story of continuous rebirth

A hungry dragon is stirring in the Far East. Its name is Haier.

In the fall of 2012, at Haier (pronounced "higher") headquarters in Qingdao, legendary founder and CEO Zhang Ruimin, cofounder Yang Mian Mian, and other key leaders were meeting to plan the transition to organisational self-management.

At Haier's nearby Corporate Culture Centre, a giant sledgehammer — a symbol of Haier's birth in 1984 — greeted visitors. Walking through the centre and reflecting on Haier's journey, one felt the power of their story of growth from humble origins to global business legend.

According to Haier's website, Zhang, a young entrepreneur, took a post as director of Haier's precursor, the Qingdao Refrigerator Factory, in 1984. At the time, the company was drowning in debt and only produced about 10,000 refrigerators each year, with terrible quality. Workers were so unkempt and dysfunctional that Zhang had to stop them from urinating on the shop floor. In frustration, he lined up 76 defective refrigerators, handed out sledgehammers to the workers, and issued a command: "Destroy them!" Zhang himself smashed one of the refrigerators to drive home his key point: the existing culture must be demolished and replaced.[7] Out of this primal act of catharsis, the modern Haier Group was born.

Named by Forbes as one of the world's 100 most powerful women,[8] Haier cofounder and president Yang shared a keen interest with Zhang in the practicalities of self-managed organisational governance. As the key person responsible for corporate strategy and management policy, she voiced thoughtful questions that reflected her intense curiosity about finding the proper balance of workplace freedom and accountability.

Today, Haier is the world's largest home-appliance manufacturer, with global revenues exceeding US$32 billion and profits of US$2.4 billion in 2014.[9] Haier's 70,000[10] employees run global operations, including 10 R&D centres, seven industrial parks, 24 manufacturing plants, and 24 trading companies.[11] To manage its sprawling enterprises, Haier created a localization mode of "three in one", which combines design, manufacture, and sales to provide ongoing support for global brand development. Boston Consulting Group called Haier one of the 10 most innovative companies in the world, and the most innovative company in the consumer and retail categories.[9] It is a true global powerhouse.

What makes it so unique?

Haier is a master of strategy. Zhang, Yang, and their team have arguably displayed some of the finest strategic business thinking on the planet over the last three decades. Jim Stengel, former global marketing officer of Proctor & Gamble and author of *Grow: How Ideals Power Growth and Profit at the World's Greatest Companies*, chose Zhang as head of strategy for a dream team composed of world's finest business leaders.[12]

Haier's results have been nothing short of spectacular. According to the its website, the company grew from a small money-losing operation in 1984 to achieve global revenue of 188.7 billion yuan in 2015 and total profit of 18 billion yuan with 20% year-on-year growth.[13] Euromonitor International named Haier, with its 9.8% global market share by retail volumes,119 the top major-appliance brand in the world for the seventh consecutive year in 2015. Even in 2013's sluggish economy, the company posted sales growth of 14%.117 The Haier name is universally known in China and is one of relatively few Chinese brands with global recognition. Haier opened the first Chinese-owned factory in the US in South Carolina in 2000 to manufacture refrigerators for the American market.[14]

As Zhang told the BBC's Peter Day:[15]

> *I believe in getting the best of both worlds, both from Chinese culture and from the West. The good thing about Chinese culture is that it treats something as a whole system, the forest not just the trees. You can see this in the difference of approach of traditional Chinese medicine and Western medicine. Western medicine treats symptoms; traditional Chinese medicine treats the whole body, holistically. Western culture wants everything quantified... so we have also adopted some Western management concepts.*

Haier organizes around core values. According to Haier's website, its success rests on three of those values.[16] The first value is "Users are always right; we need to improve ourselves." Haier believes that this is the driving force to create value for users. The second value is that the twin spirits of entrepreneurship and innovation are at the heart of Haier culture. This value envisions the shift in mindset from being a managed worker to embracing the possibility, however challenging, of becoming the CEO of an entirely new enterprise. The third value is the idea of the ZZJYT, shorthand for *zi zhu jing ying ti*,[17] which translates to "independent operating units" — self-managed teams.

So exactly what does a ZZJYT look like, anyway?

Seismic wave of change

Zhang is extraordinarily well read. From Peter Drucker, he learned that employees realise their value by making decisions (in his presentation at the 2015 Global Drucker Forum, he described his vision of *rendanheyi* — connecting employees directly with end users).[18] From Immanuel Kant, he learned that human beings should be treated as ends rather than as means.[19] And from Clay Shirky, author of *Here Comes Everybody: The Power of Organizing without Organizations,* he learned about the power of the Internet to collapse distances between customers and suppliers — and between managers and workers. Haier had been organized into a traditional hierarchy, with silos for R&D, finance, and the rest. Information was supposed to flow up and down the chain of command to create ultimate value for customers.

In 2009, Haier's visionary leader had had enough. He retooled the organisation to radically empower self-managed teams. Workers would have information about customers and markets via the Internet. All workers would be free to develop an innovative idea — for example, a new refrigerator model. If he or she could sell management on the idea, that worker would be given the chance to recruit and lead their own project team staffed with subject-matter experts attracted to the idea, who would then receive a share of any profits.

By the end of 2012, Zhang had eliminated most middle management, allowing the self-managed teams, the multidisciplinary ZZJYTs, to flourish — which they did, quickly growing to some 2,000 teams. The sheer size and scale of the move was breath-taking — Zhang clearly believed that the risk of standing still far outweighed the risk of radical change. He did, however, recognize the risk of a system in constant upheaval. For example, organisational self-managers could organically shift back and forth between teams, which would form and then dissolve like the clouds over Qingdao harbour.

"I have to find a balance between reform and risk," Zhang has said.[7] One of Haier's inspirations is Morning Star, which began practicing organisational self-management in 1990.[12] "The most difficult thing is that in the past the employees would listen to their bosses, but now they don't have any bosses; they have to listen to the users," Zhang has observed.[15] His goal for Haier's self-managed teams is to create zero distance to the customer.

Haier America has begun implementing the reforms, and Zhang intends to extend worldwide his vision of a company full of self-organizing entrepreneurs. As he said to Forbes contributor Jim Stengel in 2012, the future of organisation design will be more self-managed.[12]

Challenges

No disruptive change effort is without challenges.

First, in moving to a flat, self-managed ecosystem, Haier laid off 4,000 middle managers. The company invited many to reapply, but for entrepreneurial positions in the new, flatter company.

Second, Haier experienced a quantum of employee unhappiness as a result of the massive change. As Zhang noted:

> *This is a really difficult nut to crack. The only thing we can do is provide employees with a level playing field, where they can compete on an equal footing for opportunities within the company. In reality, however, even this isn't good enough; many employees just don't have the necessary skills. So, what do we do? This is an issue we have yet to fully resolve.*

The third challenge lies in the sheer borderless-ness of Haier's web-based ecosystem. Not only are there no borders between stakeholders (customers, suppliers, universities, competitors, experts, etc.), but Haier's leaders have had to rethink their entire business. As Zhang stated:

> ...We believe that there is no "inside" the company versus "outside" anymore. As a Haier executive, my goal is no longer to be a maker of home appliances, but to be an agent of interaction and networking among people who might be anywhere. I want to turn the company into an Internet-based company, a company unrestricted by borders. Whoever is capable, come and work with us.

Haier's relentless effort to resolve these challenges continues.

Power of the Haier platform

Haier's powerful Internet platform allows limitless collaboration with suppliers, customers, universities, competitors, the public, and multiple other stakeholders.

When the company entered the water-purification business, it learned that consumers were more likely to buy water-filtering equipment while using Haier's impressive website to customize household-appliance purchases. Haier trained its consultants to research complex details about water quality by neighbourhood and to install proper filters for the specific pollutants in a given area. The company created even more value by posting water-quality data for 220,000 communities in China on its website.[20]

In this example and others, Haier showcases stakeholder integration of the highest order, coupled with stellar organisational performance. Haier also demonstrates that individuals are never a means to an end, but the reason for one's existence in the first place.

From its humble beginnings with 76 sledgehammers to the present-day workplace of the future (and recent purchaser of GE Appliances123), Haier is finally acquiring the reputation for innovation and excellence it richly deserves — in its products, services, and organisational design.

The dragon is rising.

PART TEN

Funding #noprojects

It helps those of you reading this who aren't from a finance background to approach the subject of funding with empathy and understanding, to understand that there is an important reason for the processes and controls that the CFO places on an organisation.* Fundamentally, finance are accountable for the management of all fiscal elements of the business. And they are held to account for the correct allocation of every dollar by many masters: the CEO, the board, shareholders, external auditors, the legislative taxation body, and corporate regulators.

The finance domain includes:

- typical products like an annual report, budget allocation, and tax filings;
- typical processes like cashflow management, managing accounts, shares management, short-term and long-term investments, managing depreciable assets, and raising capital (shares and loans);
- optional processes like procurement, forex markets and currency conversion, and international trade; and
- frameworks and guidelines like relevant tax and accounting legislation, GAAP, CPA, or equivalent guidelines.

We explain this because it's important to understand what finance needs from you — not what they ask for, but what they really need. In a word, that is predictability.

If you've been paying attention, you know that this entire book is predicated on the fact that we live in an unpredictable (or VUCA) world. Historically, projects have given finance a false sense of predictability. The business case and project plan make a promise to finance: for $X, you'll get Y in return. And historically, we've broken that promise more often than not. Is it any wonder that finance keeps putting stricter controls on the entire organisation to try to gain that financial predictability?

We are going to let you in on a little secret: funding a continuous stream of work without the false security of a project is both simpler and more predictable for you, your customer, and your finance division. From personal experience, and without exception, we've had positive feedback from the finance teams in every organisation where we've worked to embed a #noprojects approach.

---

* And the more complex and organisation, the more controls are needed.

While writing this book, we spent a lot of time discussing what we should call it. One title that we played around with for quite a while* was *Continuous Flow*. While we have to admit that it isn't a good title, it capably describes what #noprojects is, how funding works, and why it gives finance easier forecasts and predictability. For finance, #noprojects means working with a predictable and linear spending curve that can scale on demand.

GAAP explained

Let us take a moment to explain some of the core principles behind financial accounting. If you're going to have a conversation about moving towards funding teams based on #noprojects approaches, you're going to have to be able to speak finance's language.

There is a set of finance principles called the generally accepted accounting principles, or GAAP for short — although, do note that there are multiple competing (if similar) standards across the world (e.g., IFRS and IAS). GAAP is made up of four basic principles and five basic constraints that are designed to remove subjectivity and bias from corporate accounts.

Principles

1. **Historical-cost principle** — Companies account for and report the acquisition costs of assets and liabilities rather than their fair market value.[2]
2. **Revenue-recognition principle** — Companies record revenue when earned rather than when received. This is the essence of accrual accounting.
3. **Matching principle** — Where reasonable, expenses have to be matched with revenues and must be recorded in the same accounting period as the revenue it helped to earn. Only if no connection with revenue can be established may it be charged as expenses to the current period.
4. **Full-disclosure principle** — Information disclosed should be enough to make a judgment while keeping preparation costs reasonable.

---

* That obviously didn't make it.

Constraints

5. **Objectivity principle** — Financial statements provided by accountants should be based on objective evidence such that different people looking at the same information will arrive at the same conclusions.
6. **Materiality principle** — The significance of an item should be considered when it is reported. An item is considered significant when it would affect the decision of a reasonable individual.
7. **Consistency principle** — The company uses the same accounting principles and methods from period to period.
8. **Conservatism principle** — Accounting should be fair and reasonable and should never overstate or understate the affairs of the business or the results of operation.

Cost constraint — The benefits of reporting financial information should justify and be greater than the costs imposed on supplying it.

It comes down to how work is planned, measured, and executed in a #noprojects or continuous-delivery model. A traditional project is funded based on the estimated effort and duration of a fixed scope of work (which is often incorrect[*]) and where the benefits are usually measured after the project is complete. #noprojects initiatives are funded based on a steady rate of financial spend (the aforementioned stable value-delivery team) against a regularly measured business outcome (the aforementioned outcome profile). The return on investment remains an assumption but the period of measure is exponentially shorter. By dynamically planning, prioritising, and monitoring activities against outcomes, teams can manage their budgets and deliver the highest-value activities first.

Because we have greater predictability and can focus on value realisation rather than on measuring outputs, we're in a much stronger position to demonstrate value to customers and shareholders. Nowhere is this more evident than at the start of a "project". In our previous lives as project managers, we would often spend up to four months writing business cases to justify ROI before we could start a project.[†] Now, we have teams who are funded by outcome (not by work) so we can start with a hypothesis, an

---

[*] Ultimately, if we had perfect estimation, we wouldn't be writing this book.
[†] Which was always frustrating because the project was already funded in the annual plan — we just had to do the dance to find the right words in the business case to make finance happy so that they would release the already allocated funds.

assumption of value, and spend those same months demonstrating ROI. And if our assumption is wrong, we can make an informed decision to stop, pivot, or continue.[*]

The question that always gets asked of us is what about capex and opex? The elegant simplicity of #noprojects helps provide a simple answer to this as well. The trick is to determine which class of activities contribute to a capital asset and which do not.

Capex explained

The world of corporate finance is complex and requires more depth than we can give here. However, there are a few key concepts you need to understand to have this conversation. Foremost is to understand capitalisation.

In brief, many of the "things" we create have value over multiple years. We call these assets. If I cook myself a delicious dinner, its value lasts for a couple of hours.[†] If I buy a new oven that lets me cook many meals, the value of that oven lasts for decades.

We want companies to create capital assets because this is what drives long-term economic development and generally creates a sustainable revenue stream. The downside is that it costs a lot of money up front to build an asset and it can take several years to recoup that investment. The implication of this is that companies want to be able to spread the impact of that initial loss out over the lifespan of the asset[‡] (for both tax and accounting purposes).

It's also important to understand that the value in capital assets changes over time. Some will depreciate (that new car you purchased will never be worth more than when you first bought it[§]) and others will appreciate (your house is probably worth more than when you bought it). Some assets will earn you money while you own it (a rental property) and the value of others is only realised when you sell it (your home).

---

[*] If delivering the outcome is more important than the ROI.
[†] And maybe a couple of weeks around my waist
[‡] Ironically, longer than any initial project.
[§] Well, it might be if you had actually bought that new Lotus in 1974 and kept it in pristine condition until today.

So, the rules are clear. For an asset to be capitalisable, it has to have a useful life beyond one year, have clear business value (e.g., directly or indirectly helps you generate income), and be something you own. Within those criteria, anything can be an asset, including an intangible object like software.

So, when spending money or effort, a capital expense (usually shortened to "capex") is anything that materially contributes to the creation of an asset and an operational expense ("opex") is anything that contributes to running the business.

///

To determine which activities are capex and which are opex, always start by talking with your finance department. They will be able to work with you to develop clear guidelines that are in compliance with industry standards and relevant taxation legislation and will withstand an external audit. In general, there are some common principles at play:

- First, the product has to be something that generates value over multiple years. HR or marketing teams will be nearly 100% opex — a marketing campaign or HR policy is not an asset. The acquisition of physical hardware or plant equipment will nearly always be 100% capex.

- In developing a product, the work of most roles can be capitalised. In a software team, the costs of the time spent by developers, testers, architects, and designers are all capitalisable. Some organisations (depending on country and company policy) will capitalise the costs of ScrumMasters and management roles while others will not. Administrative support and training is always opex.

- In enhancing* a product, most work can be capitalised. In that same software team, all effort going towards creating a new feature, extending existing features to reach new users (internationalisation or multiplatform development), and improving the existing code base (e.g., refactoring, performance, or DR) would be capex. However, there are many activities you cannot capitalise. Temporary customis-

---

* In an early draft of this book, we had used the phrase "in maintaining a product". I was (rightly) slapped down for this (thanks Pat Reed). While we were using the term to imply a continuous flow of new features and improvements, the word maintenance has a very explicit expense connotation to auditors, finance teams and accountants. Hence the term, enhancements.

ations, feasibility spikes, and resolving defects (from production, not in the usual day-to-day development) would be opex.

And it's pretty easy to track. Once you have a clear understanding of the characteristics, tools like an agile backlog or the activity canvas can be used to differentiate between capex and opex. And it doesn't have to be complicated — if you're using a physical board, then using different-coloured sticky notes is sufficient. However, as audits are usually done long after the work is complete, care needs to be taken to keep appropriate evidence. This is where electronic tools have the advantage. Electronic tools generally allow you to classify all activities[*] by type and, if you've predetermined which type is capex and which is opex, you're almost done. The final step is to clearly record when the work was released[†] into the market so that the finance teams can accurately track the depreciation & value of the total asset.

Once you've got the percentage of capex and opex work by team, that information can feed into both forecasts and actual reports.

Some organisations will create 100% capex or opex teams in which team members work on either only capital or operational work. The traditional build teams and run teams would fall under this format. We do not recommend this as it breaks many of the principles of #noprojects: those of cross-functional and outcome-focused teams. While some outcomes may be purely opex, it would be incredibly rare for an outcome that requires capital development not to also require operational investment.

We also caution against tracking work by hours.[‡] That level of granularity introduces additional complexity and interruptions into the workflow of teams, with the associated reduction in productivity. Luckily, we have many other measures on our toolbelt that satisfy both finance and external auditors. Two common measures are velocity and cycle time.

Velocity is a relative measure used by many agile teams. It is simply calculated as the number of story points delivered in a defined unit of time (usually a two-week iteration). A story point is a relative estimate of effort. Say that activity A is twice as hard as activity B. So, if A is given a relative value of 2, then B must be 4. The advantage is that velocity correlates with actual effort and is automatically calculated at the end of every iteration. It can also be independently verified based on the data that

---

[*] Or story, ticket, card, etc… — pick your metaphor.
[†] Or deployed, launched, etc… — there are plenty of metaphors to choose from.
[‡] Let's face it, nobody likes timesheets.

both finance and auditors require. One piece of advice here; story points, by themselves, are generally not accurate enough for financial reporting. You must ensure that the velocity is accurately correlated to effort and time at the end of the iteration.

A second measure, coming out of lean, is cycle time. Rather than creating an estimate, cycle time is simply the average of how long each specific activity takes to deliver to the customer (or a predefined endpoint). This works best with an automated tool and when activities aren't too small (between half a day and two days is ideal). Once again, this measure can be independently verified based on the data.

However, regardless of the approach used, the goal is to be able to prepare for, and pass, a capitalisation audit – an independent validation that the allocation of capital and operational expenses were valid. If you can't pass the audit with flying colours, you run the risk of having to pay penalties and re-report earnings[*].

We also need to measure value delivered against the target outcomes. Focusing just on capex and opex leads to the same behaviours as measuring time, cost, and scope in a project. While each value-delivery team will define unique measures against each outcome profile, there are certain common value-based measures you[†] should consider:

- quality (e.g., defect injection rate, MTTR,[‡] number of failed units, percentage of returns, etc.),
- customer and employee engagement and satisfaction (e.g., NPS[§]),
- organisation responsiveness,
- experimentation and learning,
- effectiveness (doing the right work), and
- balancing productivity with efficiency (doing the work right).

There's an interesting nuance in talking about measuring productivity versus efficiency. Many organisations focus on efficiency as a way of driving down costs, which it does. However, once again, that's not what

---

[*] which is never a good thing for investor confidence or shareholder trust
[†] And your finance team.
[‡] Mean time to repair.
[§] We personally dislike NPS ("How likely are you to recommend us?") as it can be easily gamed. We'd prefer to ask a simpler yes-or-no question like "Have you recommended us?"

is most important. With apologies, let us explain this with some mathematics.[*]

```
r = (P/C)*100
```

Efficiency (r) is the total amount of useful product output (P) produced against the cost of resources[†] consumed (C). In a business sense, this is the profit margin.

```
p = O/I
```

Productivity (p) is the ratio of the business output (O) to key inputs (I; in this case we're using a single-factor productivity calculation). In a business sense, this is the total profit.

So, let's create an example. Pretend you run a marketing organisation with two value-delivery teams who create advertising campaigns for your clients. Let's say you sell every campaign for $10,000.

The first value-delivery team of five junior marketers takes one week to produce a campaign with a total cost of $5,000. This gives you a profit per person of $1,000.

Efficiency	Productivity	Profit per person
P = 10000	O = 1	(10000 - 5000) * 0.2 =
C = 5000	I = 5	$1000
r = 10000/5000 = 200%	p = 0.2	

The second, senior team (also five people) costs $8,000 per week but produces three campaigns in the same time.

Efficiency	Productivity	Profit per person
P = 10000	O = 3	(10000 - 8000) * 0.6 =
C = 8000	I = 5	$1200
r = 10000/8000 = 125%	p = 0.6	

You see in this instance that even though the first team is more efficient (200% versus 125%), the second team makes more profit ($1,000 versus $1,200 per person). Beyond this simple example, the problem is that productivity is hard to truly define and efficiency is easy to calculate. So, if

---

[*] We're taking a very simplistic approach to give you an idea of how it works. It's much, much, much more complicated in reality.
[†] Yet again, people aren't resources — but try telling that to mathematicians.

profits are down, it's easier to focus on efficiency at the expense of productivity.

There's one more element around funding #noprojects to cover, and that's governance. It may surprise you, but we are big fans of governance*. The key is to build the right level of governance proportionate to the risk in a way that doesn't slow down work. Before we proceed, let's quickly refresh some basic principles of #noprojects:

- We have trusted and empowered teams.
- Teams are built around business outcomes.
- We measure outcomes on a regular basis.
- Teams pull the work to themselves.

In this context, the question to ask is what is the most appropriate governance with the lightest possible touch? To answer that, we need to introduce you to the two basic types of corporate governance: approval and audit.

Approval-based governance is a gate or a checkpoint. It says, "Stop here while we'll check to make sure you can proceed." This form of governance is appropriate in high-risk or high-cost environments, especially in situations where the cost/impact of failure is high — when there is a risk of death, injury, or significant financial cost. For example, when building your house, you're going to stop and check that the foundations are right before you continue to build anything else.

Audit-based governance checks that you are doing the right work and that you are doing it right. It says, "Keep going, and we'll check in with you every couple of weeks." This form of governance is appropriate in lower-risk or time-critical situations, which is pretty much every situation not included above.

What about situations that are both high risk and time critical? In these cases, it comes down to the operating† context. If you're bleeding out, you want the doctor to fix your injury professionally and quickly, without waiting for external approval. If there's a little more time, you'd like the doctor to please stop and check that they're operating on the right‡ leg.

---

* In fact, the name of Evan's first book was almost "Agile Corporate Governance". No one is suggesting that he is good with names.
† Pun intended.
‡ Or left.

If it's not obvious which form of governance applies, we prefer audit-based governance to approval-based governance in most #noprojects environments. It allows teams to work at speed while providing confidence that when mistakes* occur, they can be identified and corrected quickly with "a small blast radius".[1]

How much does this cost? This is the question that every project manager is asked at some point. We hope that by this time you realise that it's the wrong question. The real question is: **What is it worth?**

Everything we've spoken about so far comes down to these four words. We are near the end of the book, and these four words are probably the most important four words yet written in it. If you can't answer this question, you need to have a good look at the work that you are doing. If you can't even *ask* this question, you've got a serious cultural problem inside your organisation. In our experience, there is really only one situation where this question is hard to both ask and answer: external vendor contracts.

Writing a contract with a vendor in a #noprojects environment can be incredibly difficult. To clarify, we're not talking about a contract for specific goods (use a price per widget or fixed price) or contracts for individual contractors (use time and materials); those don't really change. But when you're contracting a third party to deliver work or a product for you, the traditional contract of fixed price, time, and scope won't work. That's partly because the work is highly variable but also because you have designed your teams around delivering outcomes.

Fundamentally, a contract is defined by the level of risk each party is willing to accept. To manage this risk, there are three questions that every organisation will ask at some point:

1. How much will this cost?
2. How long will it take?
3. What am I going to get?

And while "as much as you're willing to spend", "as long as necessary", and "whatever you ask for" are sometimes acceptable answers, many organisations are uncomfortable with this approach. This reflects more on the organisation than the vendor but has often led to the misconception that teams are writing themselves blank cheques.

---

* Or, sadly, fraud.

Let's first be clear about the basics. There is a fundamental relationship between time, cost, and scope. To understand this, it can help to visualise any work as a pipe. The width of the pipe is your team size, the length of the pipe is the time available to deliver, and the flow is your scope. If you're engaging a vendor team as a #noprojects team, then time is not really a constraint. However, if you're engaging them to provide short-term services within a wider #noprojects environment, it may be.

Therefore, any variations require one of these three variables to change. Effectively, and simplistically, you have three options: increase capacity (cost), increase duration (time), or drop requirement (scope).

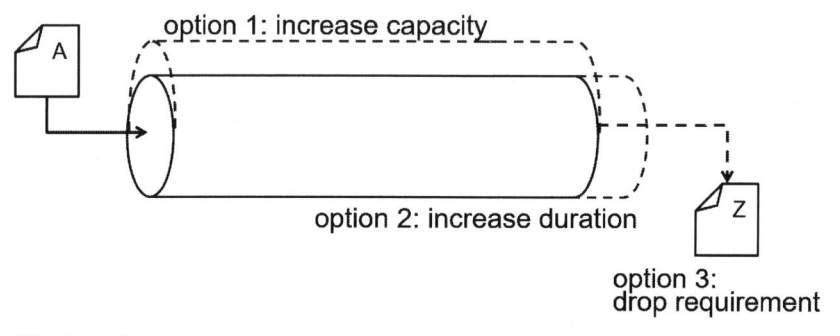

The iron pipe.

Overtime isn't a solution, as current research[2] suggests[3] that long-term[4], sustained[5] overtime leads to a significant reduction in productivity. Neither is "reducing quality" to somehow go faster – we know the impact of technical debt and the falsehood that doing shoddy work takes less time.

So, what does this mean for contracts? Traditional contracts rely on predictability — I'll pay you X to do Y — which demonstrates a fundamental flaw in how you traditionally build contracts. So, you need to find a different constraint, a different way of agreeing to a commitment. Experience shows that most software contacts come in three forms: time and materials, outcome based, or fixed contracts.

Time and materials (T&M) is the most agile contract model and provides the greatest flexibility to change, scale, and adapt on demand. If you are able to identify and prioritise the value of any unit of work, a T&M contract gives you the flexibility to stop work (or at least trigger the contract closure clauses) when the cost of delivery is greater than the value of what is delivered. In other words, work should continue until you choose to stop.

—Cost vs. --Value

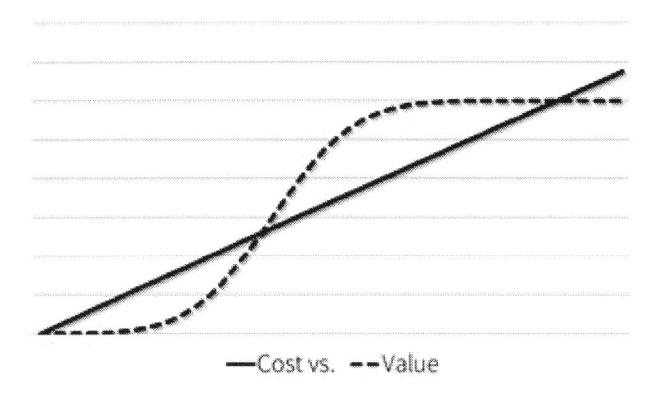

To understand what this means, it can help to visualise the rate of spend. In the above figure, we track the value of work against a linear financial spend (fixed team size). In this example, the initial work is of low value,[*] followed by low-effort yet high-value tasks, followed by the lower-value and harder tasks. This is the exact model used in the activity canvas. In this case, it is very easy to see where the T&M contract should come to an end as the value diminishes against the cost.

If you need additional controls, you can create a capped T&M contract, which limits financial spend to a fixed amount. It's important to ensure that the cap is high enough so that the overall return on investment is positive. You can also introduce a guaranteed minimum spend or delivery bonuses to encourage productivity in the team.[†]

Outcome-based or performance-based contracts are gaining popularity. These are sometimes known as "power by the hour" in reference to the support contracts for aircraft engines that are based on hours flown rather than fixed or annualised contracts.

The terms and measures in this contract should directly relate to the outcomes defined in the outcome profile. However, do not underestimate the difficulty inherent in agreeing on a mutually acceptable financial model. Common examples of outcome-based contracts are software as a service and other pay-per-use models.

In the contract, and alongside the outcome profile, you'll also need to define the payment curve (how will you pay, or be paid, against the performance measures), incentives to exceed the baseline measure, and the acceptable level of risk to the outcome.

---

[*] But necessary to enable the later, high-value pieces of work to be done at all.
[†] However, be wary of incentivising the wrong behaviour.

Mirko Kleiner[6] has an approach he calls "lean-agile procurement", which uses a lean procurement canvas to identify shared goals and outcomes, find alignment on the way of working, and rapidly agree to either work with a vendor or part ways.

Sadly, many organisations will still require fixed contracts, especially where there are significant capital costs. In a traditional project, this would be a combination of fixed cost, time, or scope. In the worst case, all three would be fixed. Providing fixed quotes can sometimes be compatible with #noprojects but this requires careful attention to manage the flexible component in a way that is reasonable and achievable.

- **Fixed cost** — This is a capped contract where the vendor provides services up to a price. What they do and how long it takes is completely flexible.

- **Fixed time** — If a specific unit of work needs to be done in a specific time frame, a fixed-time contract may be appropriate.

- **Fixed cost and time** — This is the most common type of fixed contract in a #noprojects environment: a contracted team, supplementing the existing team, hired for a limited period of time at a fixed cost.

Where possible, avoid fixed scope in any combination unless the work is short or obvious.* In place of scope constraints, incorporate other constraints into the contract terms. For example:

- quality constraints (e.g., defect injection rate),
- MTTR (mean time to recover),
- ROI (maintaining a positive effort-to-value ratio, similar to the T&M example above),
- MVP (minimum viable product; a limited scope constraint that should be no more than 20% of the total contract size), or
- productivity improvements (a small, incremental increase in productivity measures over time).

All these approaches fundamentally come down to the core principle of managing risk. Your contract terms are going to be set by the level of risk each party is willing to accept. In a #noprojects context, avoid a contract that overly constrains a partnership where the risk is already low or is acceptable.

---

* We're using the Cynefin definition of obvious here.

There is one final factor, for both finance teams and contracts, that needs to be understood: trust. As we have demonstrated, you operate in an unpredictable environment, bordering on chaotic, and customers (whether external or internal) traditionally try to establish control through constraining scope. #noprojects, on the other hand, is successful because it takes advantage of (rather than controls) this unpredictability.

However, you come up against your customers' natural concerns and fears. Can they trust you to act in their best interest? Can they trust you to fail fast? If you can't guarantee exactly what they'll get, can they trust you to deliver something of value? The less your customers trust you, the less responsive you can be.

The form and flexibility of the relationship between parties depends on the level of trust that exists between them. We define this across four distinct levels:[*]

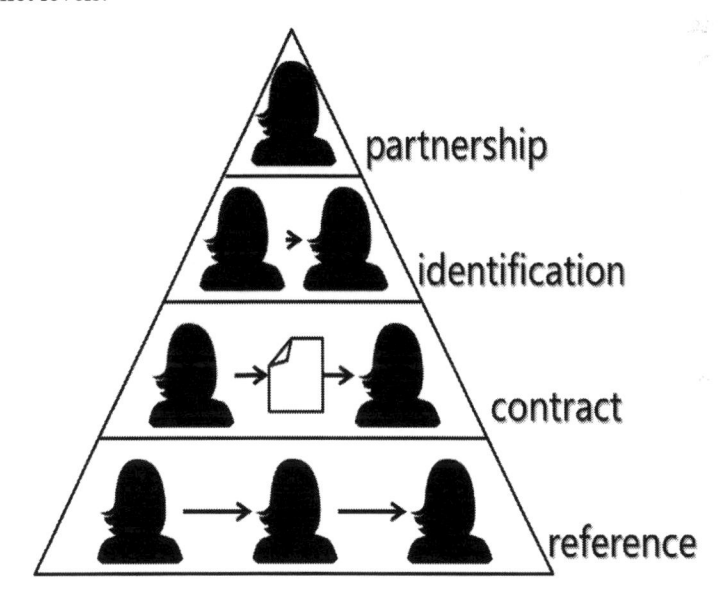

Trust pyramid.

---

1. **Reference** — This is the lowest form of trust and exists where trust between the parties is based on the reference of a mutually trusted third party.

---

[*] In Evan's first book, he described five layers of trust (reference, contract, knowledge, identification, and team). However, the distinction between knowledge and identification was confusing, so we've merged them.

2. **Contract** — This is the most common level of trust, and the majority of relationships do not extend beyond this. This exists where parties create legally binding contracts (potentially with penalty clauses) as the core mechanism to enable trust between them.

3. **Identification** — This level of trust evolves over time and exists where parties have the opportunity to work together and build trust based on personal experiences. This is where we can really start to be agile.

4. **Partnership** — This is the highest level of trust and exists when both parties share the same goals and outcomes. This may take the form of a strategic partnership or similar structure.

How do you build trust? Being trustworthy is a good start. Act with fairness and integrity, share knowledge, be transparent, and of course perform competently. Within teams, leaders who delegate outcomes (rather than actions), explain why, seek and value opinions, celebrate success, and give everyone opportunities to contribute (but still consider group rather than individual interests) build trust with their teams. It's also worth mentioning that trust is based on perception rather than reality (in an ideal world, perception and reality would be the same). Acting with confidence and displaying concern or empathy are good ways to build trust at the start of a relationship.

CASE STUDY
Evolving budget management
by Joanna L. Vahlsing

When the product-development organisation within a leading health company moved to adopt more agile approaches, the shift required that the transition team determine how to ensure that annual budgeting still met the needs of the finance organisation and that the process would help to build an investment mindset to replace the fixed-project-budget mindset.

This case study covers the challenges of the previous model, the evolution of budget management, and the benefits that the organisation saw once the changes were in place.

Problems

The organization was facing two main problems.

First, the annual budgeting process required that all project, program, and portfolio planning be completed up front for the following year, effectively locking in the plan and preventing the adoption of opportunities and changes based on market conditions and consumer feedback.

Next, the process created a mindset in which projects needed to be completed and the budget spent, regardless of whether or not the project still provided value, leading to decreased agility due to scarce resources (resources were tied up in approved projects).

Also, the project-budgeting process created tension over project scope amongst decision makers and the team delivering the work because if they did not deliver the scope within the budget or time window, all would lose their opportunity to get what they wanted.

Another problem was the overhead that went into managing the budget and resourcing, which in lean terms mostly created waste and re-work due to the granularity with which the budget had to be managed. For capitalisation purposes, team members needed to track their time spent on each task and in which stage the work was undertaken (requirements, design, build, test, or release).

Causes

As with most organisations, there is a requirement to create an annual budget. When the organisation was working in a waterfall approach, planning for the following year would begin to take place in Q4. In this particular process, the heads of each business function would make a presentation to the executive team and compete to have their projects approved for the plan.

Once a project was placed into the bucket of worthwhile projects, the PMO would start to work with the leaders of the product-development organisation to meticulously plan which and how many resources* would be needed for how long.

The waterfall methodology resulted in a sequenced plan that had those working on requirements for Project 1 finished just in time to start on the requirements for Project 2, with the same applied to the design, build, test, and release stages.

The draft plan would go through a variety of versions until it was locked down and sent to the finance team, who would apply personnel costs and create the annual operating budget. This would then be revised (usually down). Once the draft met the target spend amount, it was then set as the annual operating plan.

The project manager was responsible for assembling the resources and starting the project at the planned time. Most people assigned to the project had not been involved in the decision to put it in the annual operating plan so most kickoffs started with a couple of line-item notes from the executive planning meeting the year before. Outcome ownership and team-member engagement usually did not exist.

Without some level of outcome ownership, most project team members didn't stop to think if the project would still bring the same level of value it had been thought to bring when it was discussed in annual planning.

Solution

In the agile transformation, the product-development organisation moved from project teams to durable product teams, with each team focused on and owning one particular area of the product. These teams had all the skills that they would need to deliver their outcomes, including product management embedded in the team. They were also tasked with goals

---

* This means people. See our earlier point about humans not being resources!

that were outcomes instead of specific projects or features. One example of a goal was that the team responsible for the digital sign-up funnel had to increase paid conversions by some percentage.

To support this, the budgeting process also needed adjustment. While there would continue to be an annual plan, that plan would look different than it did in the waterfall days. The plan included outcomes instead of features/products and durable teams focused on achieving those ongoing outcomes.

We also had teams dedicated to investigating and testing out ideas. We would invest the team members' time for a period, assess the investment's performance, and decide if we wanted to continue to invest in that test or move the team to the next test.

The smallest increment the organization would plan in would be a team.

This approach created flexibility for what team members were working on, encouraged them to try new things if outcomes were unsatisfactory, increased ownership and engagement, and prevented the "we have the money budgeted so we must spend it all" mindset.

The approach also provided finance with the information they needed to set the annual plan while maintaining clarity regarding who was working on what and what can be capitalized.

Implementation
Because the executive team supported the transition to more agile ways of working, success came down to how finance would buy into this approach.

Finance team members were involved in the transition from the beginning. The first steps were to increase their buy-in by showing how their needs would still be met with this new process. It required educating them in the new approach to product-development planning and the benefits it would bring and working with them to ensure that there was transparency, clarity, and understanding.

We conducted a dry run with finance before setting the following year's budget and worked through any issues and questions as we created the necessary templates and artefacts.

When it came time to set the annual budget for real, planning went smoothly. The year was planned based on the rough number of teams that were needed, based on what the organization was trying to accomplish. It was easy enough to understand the product/software-development organisation's run rate, find the average cost of a team, then figure out if and when we would need to add more teams during the year.

Because using product teams instead of projects built more flexibility into the plan, budget-management overhead significantly dropped, which allowed the finance team to use that saved time to work on more strategic items.

We continued to use timesheets to track individuals' time spent on activities that could be capitalized. When making this switch at other organisations, we've implemented options such as estimation of administrative hours per role and other suggestions in the beyond-budgeting[7] model.

Challenges

Because this was almost a decade ago (before agile became more mainstream and understood), one of the biggest challenges was convincing finance team members that agile wasn't just a fad and that making these changes would ultimately help the company to meet its purpose and mission.

To overcome this, we knew we needed not only to approach the change from an educational perspective but also to demonstrate the benefits that the finance team would gain.

We found that we needed to take a hybrid approach because some work still needed to be planned in a waterfall fashion, mainly the back-office systems. Knowing this up front would have helped us structure the planning in a hybrid manner. Fortunately, we encountered this challenge early, while reviewing the entire portfolio of work, and we were able to determine which projects still needed to be planned and budgeted in a waterfall manner.

Outcome

Product teams were free of the constraints that budget planning usually places on a team. Teams were funded, or weren't, and it became the team's responsibility to understand how they're tracking to achieve their outcomes. At the executive level, strategic conversations could happen based on the outcome metrics and a product team could adjust their focus according to that information.

Gone were the days of the "we have it budgeted so let's spend it" mindset; the new mindset of the teams was "are we achieving our desired outcomes?"

The finance team members, without so much budget-management overhead, were able to work on more strategic items.

While we didn't track metrics as much as we would have liked to, we estimate that moving to this new mindset saved a minimum of six weeks each year of up-front planning when setting the annual plan and probably a least another four weeks throughout the year.

It was a win for all involved and helped the organization achieve increased agility.

PART ELEVEN

#noprojects and business agility

By this point, it should come as no surprise that we consider #noprojects to be a fundamental expression of business agility. With the emergence of a worldwide continuous culture, only high-performing, adaptable, and agile organisations will thrive in the battle for relevance.

This environment is not the strength of traditional project-based organisations that expect and depend on predictability — but #noprojects-based organisations with their focus on outcomes, value-delivery teams, and continuous work are designed to operate under these conditions. We want you to start thinking of #noprojects as the way an agile organisation structures and delivers work, with business agility being the common thread to the rest of the organisation.

If you will allow a slight detour in the narrative, we want to take a moment to explain what this means. To understand business agility is to understand the domains of business agility,[1] which is a practical model that consists of nine domains interacting across three dimensions and centres on the customer. It's not a pyramid or matrix but is rather a model of agility whose domains in each of the dimensions are equal, necessary, interrelated, and dependent on each other. No single domain supersedes or is more important than any of the others. Business agility only emerges when your organisation can embrace agile across all the domains and across all facets of your organisation.

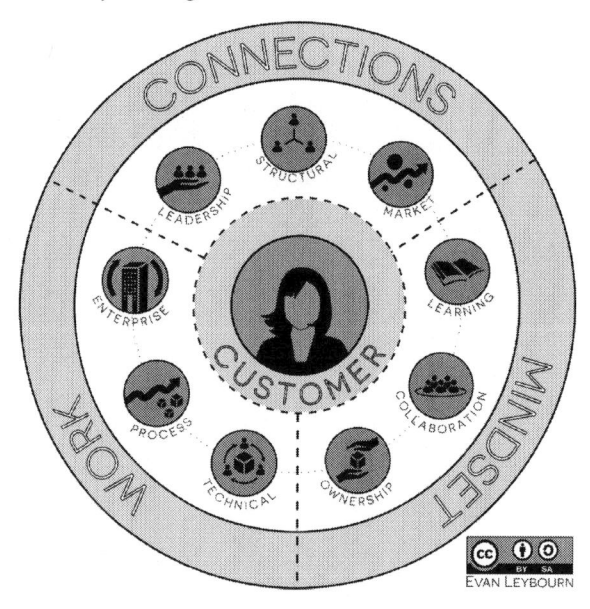

The domains of business agility.

Business agility creates purpose-driven organisations. For most companies, the customer is their purpose; in public-sector or social-good organisations, however, the definition of the customer is much broader. Regardless of how you define "customer", your customer is at the heart of the model and shapes your organisation. Surrounding the customer are the three dimensions of work, connections, and mindset:

1. The three domains in the work dimension govern how an agile organisation operates, from technical agility at the individual activity level to process agility at the value-stream level to scaling to enterprise agility at the organisation level. This is primarily where #noprojects has the greatest impact.

2. The connections dimension governs the relationships that form within and outside the organisation. Structural agility defines the relationships between individuals, teams, and divisions. Leadership agility defines the relationship with authority. Market agility defines the relationship with your users and the wider market. Value-delivery teams are the #noprojects expression of business agility in these domains.

3. The mindset dimension is concerned with governing the key characteristics of an agile organisation: a learning mindset, a collaboration mindset, and an ownership mindset.

Your customer is at the heart of business agility and is the very reason your organisation exists. "Customer" is a very broad term. Depending on your organisational context, it could mean a paying client for a private organisation, a citizen for a public-sector organisation, or an abstraction (like "the environment" or "the community") for a non-profit organisation. In some contexts, your customer may be a separate division within your organisation — although in this case, you should always consider the total value stream and the true end customer instead of just delivering to a division because of the way the reporting lines work. Regardless of who your customer is, all customers have one thing in common: they provide you with your purpose. In #noprojects, the outcomes in your outcome profiles all start with the customer.

We have placed the customer at the centre of the model[2] not only because they are the reason you do what you do, but also because customers have been invisible for so long. Look at your current org chart. Where is the customer? Organisations have said for years that customers are their most important asset and yet this asset is nowhere to be seen.

Having the customer at the centre doesn't mean that the customer is always right or that employees or shareholders aren't important. And it always remains necessary to make a profit. It simply means that almost everything that you do revolves around them. It means that they are the top of your organisation charts. It means that the work that you do, and the way that you do it, is primarily for them.

The first three domains of business agility are part of the work dimension. These three domains operate in concert to define how an agile organisation works.

Technical agility defines the techniques for delivering work, regardless of function or subject matter, in an agile way. This includes all of the techniques for continuous delivery and development that are defined in the "Continuous culture" chapter.

For decades, agile teams have promoted strong technical agility as the keystone for being agile, the purpose being to increase quality and throughput and while embracing uncertainty and change. Many of the agile methods and practices developed over the last 20 years, such as extreme programming XP, behaviour-driven development, test-driven development, and DevOps, are almost entirely devoted to technical agility. And technical agility isn't limited to software development. Any domain of work can be technically agile — for example, we're starting to see agility emerge in marketing and finance work with their own agile practices (e.g., agile marketing or beyond budgeting[3]).

To be technically agile, any work practice or technique needs to be designed for ambiguity, be customer centric, seamlessly respond to change, and promote collaboration. To benefit from technical agility, your organisation requires the other eight domains, but these techniques and practices are generally a good place to start.

Process agility is the form of agility that encompasses an individual value stream — the combination of discrete activities that teams and projects undertake. This is the form of agility that most people think of when they hear the term: agile frameworks and methods to encompass multi-step, and potentially multi-team, value streams from traditionally agile processes like software delivery to business processes. Methods such as Scrum, the Kanban method, SAFe, LeSS, disciplined agile, or lean Six Sigma are all, in large part, operating at this level (although it's true to say that many of the more complex methods operate in the enterprise agility domain as well).

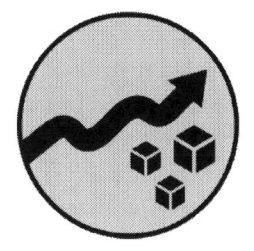

Much of #noprojects operates at this layer, as one of process agility's key elements is the focus on outcomes and products over outputs and projects. The governance of all decisions, processes, and work is directed towards ensuring the continuous delivery of value and business outcomes.

Enterprise agility scales agility across divisions, departments, the organisation, and ultimately between organisations. We are only now starting to think about enterprise agility as a discrete domain. Over the last 20 years, as individual teams became agile, the constraining factor for agility to scale was the other teams within the division. Now, as entire divisions and departments scale to become agile, the constraining factor for agility is the rest of the organisation. This is the entire point of Evan's theory of agile constraints, which we describe in the "Continuous culture" chapter. Enterprise agility emerges when there is an agile way of working across multiple teams and divisions.

The next three domains of business agility are part of the connections dimension and govern the relationships that form both within and outside the organisation. These three domains cut across the previous dimension and so, to be successful, you require elements of structural, market, and leadership agility inside each of technical, process, and enterprise agility.

Structural agility defines the relationships between individuals, teams, and divisions to create an agile organisation. The simple pyramid hierarchy no longer serves us. Laloux's teal organisation and Steve Denning's three laws[4] (laws of the small team, network, and customer) come into play across this domain. Practices such as systems thinking and the theory of constraints (including Evan's theory of agile constraints) are necessary here. At the lowest level of the organisation, these are the #noprojects value-delivery teams: small, cross-functional, and formed around business outcomes rather than traditional, skill-based, functions.

To be successful, team members need to have the four As: alignment, autonomy, authority, and accountability. Agile teams in mature organisations are self-organising and have total authority to identify their own membership and decide on the work to be done to achieve the given outcome. This demands a high level of collaboration within the team and, where appropriate, ultimately develops strong multidisciplinary members.

The connection between teams is the fundamental expression of the organisation's structure and indicates the fluency of business agility. These connections may form a hierarchical model (sometimes called "tribes") or a flatter, network model where connections form dynamically to align along the value stream. In either case, these connections group teams to business outcomes rather than to functions. Mature agile organisations break down the divisional walls even further — for example, by bringing sales and marketing, finance, or operations into the relevant cross-functional teams when needed. Guilds or centres of excellence are formed around uncommon skills (such as architecture, infrastructure, or coaching) to share expertise where and when needed.

Leadership agility defines the relationship between individuals and authority within an agile organisation. You should start thinking of everyone in the organisation as a leader whether they have institutional authority or not. Leadership models such as servant leadership or leading from the middle are part of this. While there are similarities, there is a substantial difference from traditional management, as you expect the team (including the product owner, if applicable) to decide and self-correct their own "what". Agile leaders require the ability to inspire purpose, set direction, align teams to business outcomes, remove impediments, and coach and mentor teams.

At the pioneering end of business agility and, in particular, leadership agility, there is the concept of self-organisation: teams or divisions with no managers. Although it requires a significant level of fluency across all business agility domains, self-organisation takes the position that, as Drucker[5] puts it, "every man sees himself as a 'manager' and accepts for himself the full burden of what is basically managerial responsibility: responsibility for his own job and work group, for his contribution to the performance and results of the entire organization, and for the social tasks of the work community." Without managers, self-organising teams remain aligned to company strategy and expectations by being accountable for specific, and measurable, business outcomes.

Finally, don't forget that it is agile leaders (who may not be managers) who orchestrate and guide the organisation towards business agility. These leaders help align the organisation to a single purpose, enabling individuals and teams and taking corrective action where needed.

Market agility defines the relationship between the organisation and the marketplace. Organisations have always needed to earn the right to exist in the market. However, as both market predictability and the barrier to entry are decreasing, incumbents no longer enjoy the same commercial advantage that they used to. It is agile organisations, those that frequently inspect, adapt, and pivot to meet opportunities, that are more likely to flourish in this ambiguous and uncertain market. Speed and effectiveness of this adaption to competitors, disruptors, and new customer demands are key measures of market agility.

Once you include the connection to the market in the wider systemic perspective of business agility, your view of the product lifecycle extends to include the entire value chain, from your suppliers upstream to your distributors downstream. The partnerships that this systemic perspective grants enable the creation of superior offerings that delight your customers. Methods and frameworks like lean startup, lean enterprise, design thinking, and many of the traditional agile practices fall under this domain.

The third and final dimension is concerned with addressing the cultural domains. These are the key characteristics of an agile organisation: a learning mindset, a collaboration mindset, and an ownership mindset.

Organisations with a learning mindset, those that experiment and learn faster than others, are those that succeed. Agile organisations are fundamentally learning organisations at all levels, whether the knowledge gained is small and specific (e.g., "this feature didn't sell well, so let's change it") or large and systemic ("we need to change our governance model based on this new information"). Learning is more than just observing. It's taking the observations, determining their worth, then internalising the lesson and making a new reality for the organisation.

The application of a learning mindset results in continuous improvement. Feedback loops such as "inspect and adapt" and practices such as the retrospective push teams, divisions, and organisations to improve both what they do and (more importantly) how they do it. Like the woodcutter who refuses to sharpen his axe because he has too many trees to cut down, organisations that do not improve both the way they work and their products will ultimately be out-competed in the market.

Central to the learning mindset is the ability to experiment, fail fast (with a small blast radius), and recover faster. Failure should not be seen as making a mistake but as an opportunity to learn. Organisations can make it safe to fail by recognising that failure is part of daily work and not blaming or judging people. Some organisations go further by introducing formal or informal support mechanisms like failure KPIs, parallel experiments (and selecting the best-performing option), or simply providing an environment where failure is easily identified, recognised, and rewarded.

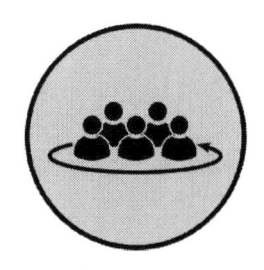

A collaboration mindset creates a culture of communication and transparency across individuals, teams, divisions, and organisations. An agile organisation is one that is designed to collaborate. The very fibre of the organisation — from the organisational structure to the work processes and even to the way they engage the market — promotes collaboration and cooperation.

The complexity of collaboration is one of the fundamental reasons teams in an agile organisation are kept small: $O(n2)$ to be precise[6] with 7±2 people a commonly accepted size. Decision making is localised to reduce the lines of communication and subsequent delays. However, don't let the goal of collaboration affect your ability to be productive. Sitting in meetings and talking is not necessarily collaboration whereas sitting quietly in a room by yourself can be.

Critical to effective collaboration is making transparency the default for information, decisions, and relationships to provide a solid foundation for trust and respect amongst customers, peers, and leaders. All individuals have the ability to know what is going on and can draw on that knowledge to make appropriate decisions. This doesn't mean that everyone knows everything but that individuals have the choice of knowing anything. And, of course, the ability to be opaque to the competition while being transparent internally is the real art of a collaboration mindset.

You can adopt many tools and practices to improve how your teams collaborate — e.g., social contracts, pair programming (or pair work outside IT), and visualisation tools (like Kanban boards, burn-down charts, or cumulative flow diagrams).

An ownership mindset means taking accountability, as an individual or team, for the quality and success of both the output and outcomes of your work. Both of these are important as ownership doesn't mean perfection. It means knowing why you are doing the work (the outcome) and making sure that what you produce (the output) is fit for the purpose. It means understanding, learning, and challenging rather than following instructions.

Teams who own their work generally take pride in what they produce. However, being agile means taking pride without arrogance. Ownership means being willing to collaborate with others — to learn from them, ask for help, even potentially reverse-engineering their work to achieve the outcome.

An ownership mindset isn't unidirectional. Individuals and teams need the authority, as well as the accountability, for an outcome. Organisations and leaders need to be transparent about their strategic decisions. For an individual or team to be held accountable for their decisions, they need to have had the appropriate information to prevent a predictably incorrect choice. This has specific implications in publicly traded organisations relating to insider-trading regulations (e.g., knowledge of share-price triggers) but many organisations have solved this conundrum.

Until such time as there is a business-agility manifesto, the values and principles of the Agile Manifesto apply across all areas of the organisation with one minor modification, in square brackets:*

> *We are uncovering better ways of delivering value by doing it and helping others do it. Through this work we have come to value:*
>
> *Individuals and interactions over processes and tools*
> *[Value creation] over comprehensive documentation*
> *Customer collaboration over contract negotiation*
> *Responding to change over following a plan*
>
> *That is, while there is value in the items on the right, we value the items on the left more.*

Keep in mind the purpose of this model: to guide you along your business-agility journey. It is #noprojects that provides the "how" while keeping you aligned to all nine domains of the model.

#noprojects is not an easy journey. The systemic nature of adopting #noprojects can have a profound impact on individuals. There must be inspiring leadership, clear communication, and a common purpose across the entire organisation to create champions out of everyone. And there will be people in your organisation who do not wish to work in this way and will leave. There's no value judgement to make; some people simply need a different way to work. Respect and understanding must be shown to everyone, even those leaving.

Despite the complexity of the transition, the benefits of #noprojects are manifest — starting with the ability to rapidly respond to competitive challenges, disruption, and changes in demand. In fact, a #noprojects organisation can do more than just respond, you can be the agent of disruption and the challenger in an uncertain and unpredictable market.

---

* Adapted from http://agilemanifesto.org/

Staff satisfaction and retention is higher and, with a general reduction in management overheads, operating costs are lower. Finally, because #noprojects starts with outcomes, you are able to be more responsive to your customers, which is the primary purpose of every organisation.

Chapter References

Part One

1. "Volatility, uncertainty, complexity and ambiguity." Wikipedia. Accessed January 9, 2018.
https://en.wikipedia.org/wiki/Volatility,_uncertainty,_complexity_and_ambiguity

2. "What Is Project Management?" PMI. Accessed February 4, 2018.
https://www.pmi.org/about/learn-about-pmi/what-is-project-management

3. Leybourn, Evan. "#noprojects — If You Need to Start a Project, You've Already Failed." InfoQ. November 18, 2015. Accessed July 18, 2016.
http://www.infoq.com/articles/noprojects1-projects-flawed

4. Kelly, Allan. *Continuous Digital*. *LeanPub*. *2017*. https://leanpub.com/cdigital/

5. Arnold, Joshua. "#NoProjects." Black Swan Farming. June 19, 2016. Accessed February 4, 2018. http://blackswanfarming.com/noprojects/

6. Smith, Steve. "No Projects." Continuous Delivery Consulting. July 28, 2013. Accessed February 4, 2018.
https://www.continuousdeliveryconsulting.com/blog/no-projects/

7. England, Rob. "IT projects go away? #NoProjects." The IT Skeptic. February 6, 2017. Accessed February 4, 2018.
http://www.itskeptic.org/content/it-projects-go-away-noprojects

8. "About." iHoriz. Accessed May 14, 2018. http://ihoriz.com/

9. Schonfeld, Erick. "Don't Be Fooled by Vanity Metrics." TechCrunch. July 30, 2011. Accessed February 4, 2018. https://techcrunch.com/2011/07/30/vanity-metrics/

Part Two

1. Weaver, Patrick. "The Origins of Modern Project Management." Fourth Annual PMI College of Scheduling Conference, Vancouver, BC. April 2007.
http://www.mosaicprojects.com.au/PDF_Papers/P050_Origins_of_Modern_PM.pdf

2. Harrison, Frederick L. and Dennis Lock. *Advanced Project Management: A Structured Approach*. *Aldershot*, England: Gower, 2004.

3. "What Is Project Management?" PMI. Accessed February 4, 2018.
https://www.pmi.org/about/learn-about-pmi/what-is-project-management

4. Defoe, Daniel. *An Essay upon Projects. 1698. Reprint, Project Gutenberg, 2014.*
http://www.gutenberg.org/files/4087/4087-h/4087-h.htm

5   Priestley, Joseph. "A Redacted Version of Priestley's *Chart of Biography (1765)*." Digital image. Wikipedia. Accessed July 18, 2016. https://en.wikipedia.org/wiki/A_Chart_of_Biography#/media/File:PriestleyChart.gif

6   Priestley, Joseph. *Lectures on History and General Policy: To Which Is Prefixed, an Essay on a Course of Liberal Education for Civil and Active Life.* London: J. Johnson, 1793. https://archive.org/details/lecturesonhis00prie

7   Playfair, William. *The Commercial and Political Atlas Representing, by Means of Stained Copper-plate Charts, the Progress of the Commerce, Revenues, Expenditure, and Debts of England, During the Whole of the Eighteenth Century.* London: J. Wallis, 1801. http://sceti.library.upenn.edu/sceti/printedbooksNew/index.cfm?TextID=hf3501_p5_1801

8   Smith, Adam. *An Inquiry into the Nature and Causes of the Wealth of Nations.* 1776. Reprint, MetaLibri, 2007. https://www.ibiblio.org/ml/libri/s/SmithA_WealthNations_p.pdf

9   Clark, Wallace. *The Gantt Chart: A Working Tool of Management.* 1923. Reprint, Internet Archive, 2007. https://ia802604.us.archive.org/26/items/ganttchartworkin00claruoft/ganttchartworkin00claruoft.pdf

10 Carayannis, Elias G., Young-Hoon Kwak, and Frank T. Anbari. *The Story of Managing Projects: An Interdisciplinary Approach.* Westport, CT: Praeger Publishers, 2005.

11 Taylor, Frederick Winslow. *Scientific Management: Comprising Shop Management, The Principles of Scientific Management.* New York: Harper, 1911.

12 Kenley, Russell and Olli Seppänen, *Location-Based Management for Construction: Planning, Scheduling and Control.* London: Routledge, 2006.

13 Johnson, Stephen B. *The Secret of Apollo: Systems Management in American and European Space Programs.* Baltimore, MD: Johns Hopkins University Press, 2006.

14 "Critical path method." Wikipedia. Accessed July 18, 2016. https://en.wikipedia.org/wiki/Critical_path_method

15 Nuggetkiwi, "Simple activity-on-node logic diagram with total float and drag computed." Digital image. Wikipedia. June 6, 2011. Accessed July 18, 2016. https://commons.wikimedia.org/wiki/File:SimpleAONwDrag3.png

16 Rouse, Margaret. "PERT Chart (Program Evaluation Review Technique)." TechTarget. May 2007. Accessed July 18, 2016. http://searchsoftwarequality.techtarget.com/definition/PERT-chart

17 Kemp, Jeremy. "PERT Chart." Digital image. Wikipedia. January 14, 2012. Accessed July 18, 2016. https://commons.wikimedia.org/wiki/File:Pert_chart_colored.svg

18 PERT Coordinating Group. *DOD and NASA Guide: PERT COST Systems Design.* Washington, DC: US Government Printing Office, 1962. https://babel.hathitrust.org/cgi/pt?id=mdp.39015006057866;view=1up;seq=1

19 Cummings, Erik G. and Kirk A. Schneider, "Cost/Schedule Control Systems Criteria: A Reference Guide to C/SCSC Information," Master's thesis. Air Force Institute of Technology, 1992. http://www.dtic.mil/dtic/tr/fulltext/u2/a258445.pdf

20 Abba, Wayne F. "How Earned Value Got to Prime Time: A Short Look Back and Glance Ahead." PMI Seminars and Symposium. 2000. Accessed July 18, 2016. http://www.evmlibrary.org/library/EVLook Back-Glance Ahead.abba.pdf

21 Dijkstra, Edsger W. "The Humble Programmer." *Communications of the ACM* 15, no. 10 (1972). https://doi.org/10.1145/355604.361591

22 Brennecke, Andreas and Reinhard Keil-Slawik, eds. *Position Papers for Dagstuhl Seminar 9635 on History of Software Engineering*. Leibniz Center for Informatics, Wadern, Germany. August 1996. https://www.dagstuhl.de/Reports/96/9635.pdf

23 Royce, Winston W. "Managing the Development of Large Software Systems." Technical Papers of Western Electronic Show and Convention (WesCon), Los Angeles. August 1970.

24 Humphrey, Watts S. *Managing the Software Process*. Reading, MA: Addison-Wesley, 1989.

25 *Insights and Trends: Current Programme and Project Management Practices*. PricewaterhouseCoopers, 2007. Accessed July 18, 2016. https://www.pwcprojects.co/Documentos/BRO%20Boosting%20Business%20Performance%20DC-07-1104-A%20v8[1].pdf

26 Beedle, Mike, et al. "Manifesto for Agile Software Development." Agilemanifesto.org. 2001. Accessed July 18, 2016. http://agilemanifesto.org/

27 "The Home of Scrum." Scrum.org. Accessed July 18, 2016. https://www.scrum.org/

28 Beck, Ken. *Extreme Programming EXplained: Embrace Change*. Reading, MA: Addison-Wesley, 2000.

29 Anderson, David J. *Kanban: Successful Evolutionary Change for Your Technology Business*. Sequim, WA: Blue Hole Press, 2010.

30 "The DSDM Agile Project Framework (2014 Onwards)." Agile Business Consortium. Accessed May 14, 2018. https://www.agilebusiness.org/resources/dsdm-handbooks/the-dsdm-agile-project-framework-2014-onwards

31 Takeuchi, Hirotaka and Ikujiro Nonaka. "The New Product Development Game." *Harvard Business Review*, January 1986. Accessed July 18, 2016. https://hbr.org/1986/01/the-new-new-product-development-game

32 Spaleka, Seweryn. "The Influence of Country of Origin on Project Management: An International Empirical Study." 19th International Scientific Conference; Economics and Management, Riga, Latvia. April, 2014.

33 Boehm, Barry W. *Software Engineering Economics*. Englewood Cliffs, NJ: Prentice-Hall, 1981.

34 Koskinen, Jussi. "Software Maintenance Costs." Working paper. Department of Computer Science and Information Systems, University of Jyväskylä, September 10, 2010. Accessed July 18, 2016. https://web.archive.org/web/20120313070806/http://users.jyu.fi/~koskinen/smcosts.htm

Part Three

1 McGrath, Rita Gunther. *The End of Competitive Advantage: How to Keep Your Strategy Moving as Fast as Your Business.* Boston, MA: Harvard Business Review Press, 2013.

2 "Employee Tenure Summary." *Economic News Releases. US Bureau of Labor Statistics.* September 22, 2016. http://www.bls.gov/news.release/tenure.nr0.htm

3 Bazigos, Michael, Aaron De Smet, and Chris Gagnon. "Why agility pays." *McKinsey Quarterly. December 2015.* http://www.mckinsey.com/business-functions/organization/our-insights/why-agility-pays

4 Leybourn, Evan. "#noprojects — If You Need to Start a Project, You've Already Failed." InfoQ. November 18, 2015. Accessed July 18, 2016. https://www.infoq.com/articles/noprojects2-focus-value

5 Flyvbjerg, Bent, and Alexander Budzier. "Why Your IT Project May Be Riskier Than You Think," *Harvard Business Review. September 1, 2011.* https://hbr.org/2011/09/why-your-it-project-may-be-riskier-than-you-think/

6 Duarte, Vasco. "NoEstimates." Software Development Today. Accessed May 10, 2018. http://softwaredevelopmenttoday.com/noestimates/

7 Zuill, Woody. "Estimation Is Easy and Useful: Estimate a Game of Chess." Life, Liberty, and the Pursuit of Agility. November 7, 2011. Accessed May 10, 2018. http://zuill.us/WoodyZuill/2011/11/07/estimation-is-easy-and-useful-estimate-a-game-of-chess/

8 Rothman, Johanna. "The Case for #NoEstimates." AgileConnection. April 22, 2015. Accessed May 10, 2018, https://www.agileconnection.com/article/case-noestimates

9 Carney, Thomas. "#NoEstimates: 6 Software Experts Give Their View on the Movement." Planio. June 14, 2016. Accessed May 10, 2018. https://plan.io/blog/noestimates-6-software-experts-give-their-view/

10 Ambler, Scott. "Surveys Exploring the Current State of Information Technology Practices." Ambysoft. Accessed April 1, 2017, http://www.ambysoft.com/surveys/

11 Basgall, Joel. "Up to 75% of Executives Anticipate Software Project Failure." Geneca. March 14, 2011. Accessed July 18, 2016. http://www.geneca.com/75-business-executives-anticipate-software-projects-fail/

12 Hastie, Shane. "Standish Group 2015 Chaos Report — Q&A with Jennifer Lynch." InfoQ. October 4, 2015. Accessed July 28, 2017. https://www.infoq.com/articles/standish-chaos-2015

13 *Securing the Value of Business Process Change. Logica Management Consulting,* October 14, 2008. Accessed July 18, 2016. https://web.archive.org/web/20101227125457/ http://www.logica.co.uk/we-are-logica/media-centre/news/2008/failing-business-process-change-projects-substantially-impact-financial-performance-of-european-bus/~/media/Global site/Imported documents/business_pro

14 Highsmith, James A. *Agile Software Development Ecosystems.* Boston, MA: Addison-Wesley, 2006.

15 Humphrey, Watts S. *PSP: A Self-Improvement Process for Software Engineers.* Boston, MA: Addison-Wesley, 2005.

16 *PMI's Pulse of the Profession: Capturing the Value of Project Management.* PMI. February, 2015. http://www.pmi.org/-/media/pmi/documents/public/pdf/learning/thought-leadership/pulse/pulse-of-the-profession-2015.pdf

17 Bloch, Michael, Sven Blumberg, and Jürgen Laartz. "Delivering large-scale IT projects on time, on budget, and on value." *Digital McKinsey.* October 2012. Accessed July 18, 2016. http://www.mckinsey.com/business-functions/business-technology/our-insights/delivering-large-scale-it-projects-on-time-on-budget-and-on-value

18 Arnold, Joshua. "Cost of Delay," Black Swan Farming. Accessed April 21, 2017. http://blackswanfarming.com/cost-of-delay/

19 Arnold, Joshua. "Qualitative Cost of Delay." Black Swan Farming. August 24, 2016. Accessed April 21, 2017. http://blackswanfarming.com/qualitative-cost-delay/

20 "An Estimated $1.6 Billion in Fraudulent Refunds Was Issued During the 2006 and 2007 Filing Seasons." Memorandum. Treasury Inspector General for Tax Administration. September 22, 2008. Accessed April 10, 2017. https://www.treasury.gov/tigta/auditreports/2008reports/200810172fr.html

21 Rothman, Johanna. "Cost of Delay: Not Shipping on Time, Part 1." Rothman Consulting Group, February 5, 2014. Accessed July 18, 2016. http://www.jrothman.com/mpd/portfolio-management/2014/02/cost-of-delay-not-shipping-on-time-part-1/

22 "Project Management." Encyclopedia of Management. Encyclopedia.com. 2009. Accessed October 1, 2016. http://www.encyclopedia.com/doc/1G2-3273100245.html

Part Four

1 Leybourn, Evan. "#noprojects — If You Need to Start a Project, You've Already Failed." InfoQ. November 18, 2015. Accessed July 18, 2016. http://www.infoq.com/articles/noprojects1-projects-flawed

2 Brougham, Greg. The Cynefin Mini-Book. InfoQ, September 19, 2015. https://www.infoq.com/minibooks/cynefin-mini-book

3. Kurtz, C. F. and D. J. Snowden. "The new dynamics of strategy: Sense-making in a complex and complicated world." *IBM Systems Journal* 42, no. 3 (2003). doi: 10.1147/sj.423.0462

4. Snowden, Dave. "Liminal Cynefin: The final cut?" Cognitive Edge. October 27, 2017. Accessed May 13, 2018. http://cognitive-edge.com/blog/liminal-cynefin-the-final-cut/

5. Leybourn, Evan. "#noprojects — Outcomes: The Value of Change." InfoQ. January 14, 2016. Accessed October 18, 2016. https://www.infoq.com/articles/noprojects3-value-change

6. Laloux, Frédéric. *Reinventing Organizations*. Brussels: Nelson Parker, 2014.

7. Ohno, Taiichi. *Toyota Production System: Beyond Large-Scale Production*. Portland, OR: Productivity Press, 2002.

8. Huckman, Robert and Bradley Staats. "The Hidden Benefits of Keeping Teams Intact." *Harvard Business Review*. December 1, 2013. Accessed July 18, 2016. https://hbr.org/2013/12/the-hidden-benefits-of-keeping-teams-intact

Part Five

1. "Value." Oxford English Dictionary. Accessed January 30, 2017. https://en.oxforddictionaries.com/definition/value

2. Hussman, David. "Dude's Law, Gordon Pask and The Shoveler." DevJam. October 5, 2010. Accessed July 18, 2016. http://devjam.com/2010/08/05/dudes-law-gordon-pask-shoveler/

3. "Confirmation bias." Wikipedia. Accessed January 30, 2017. https://en.wikipedia.org/wiki/Confirmation_bias

4. Shane Payne. "World Record 2 Hour House - Exemplary Corporate Leadership." YouTube video, 5:57. August 24, 2006. https://www.youtube.com/watch?v=I2HqW-AAb20

5. Denning, Stephen. *The Leader's Guide to Radical Management: Reinventing the Workplace for the 21st Century*. San Francisco, CA: Jossey-Bass, 2010.

6. Sheridan, Richard. *Joy, Inc.: How We Built a Workplace People Love*. New York: Portfolio/Penguin, 2013.

7. Hastie, Shane. "What Makes Joy,Inc Work? Part 3 — High-Tech Anthropology®." InfoQ. November 19, 2015. Accessed May 13, 2018. https://www.infoq.com/articles/joyinc-hightech-anthropology

8. Pixton, Pollyanna. *Stand Back and Deliver: Accelerating Business Agility*. Upper Saddle River, NJ: Addison-Wesley, 2009.

9. "Kano model." Wikipedia. Accessed January 30, 2017. https://en.wikipedia.org/wiki/Kano_model

10 Sinek, Simon. "How great leaders inspire action." Lecture, TEDxPugetSound, Newcastle, WA, September, 2009.
https://www.ted.com/talks/simon_sinek_how_great_leaders_inspire_action

Part Six

1 Kniberg, Henrik. "Spotify engineering culture (part 2)." Spotify Labs. September 20, 2014. Accessed January 9, 2018.
https://labs.spotify.com/2014/09/20/spotify-engineering-culture-part-2/

2 Senge, Peter M. *The Fifth Discipline: The Art and Practice of the Learning Organization.* New York: Doubleday, 1990.

3 Rock, David and Heidi Grant. "Why Diverse Teams Are Smarter." *Harvard Business Review.* November 4, 2016. Accessed January 9, 2018.
https://hbr.org/2016/11/why-diverse-teams-are-smarter

4 Huckman, Robert and Bradley Staats. "The Hidden Benefits of Keeping Teams Intact." *Harvard Business Review.* December 1, 2013. Accessed July 18, 2016.
https://hbr.org/2013/12/the-hidden-benefits-of-keeping-teams-intact

5 Baer, Drake. "What Multitasking Does to Your Brain." *Fast Company.* October 9, 2013. Accessed January 9, 2018.
https://www.fastcompany.com/3019659/what-multitasking-does-to-your-brain

6 Weinberg, Gerald M. *Quality Software Management.* New York: Dorset House Publishing, 1997.

7 Bogard, Jimmy. "From sprints to pull-based flow." LosTechies. May 13, 2011. Accessed January 9, 2018.
https://lostechies.com/jimmybogard/2011/05/13/from-sprints-to-pull-based-flow/

8 Schonfeld, Erick. "Don't Be Fooled by Vanity Metrics." TechCrunch. July 30, 2011. Accessed January 9, 2018. https://techcrunch.com/2011/07/30/vanity-metrics/

9 Leybourn, Evan. *Directing the Agile Organisation: A Lean Approach to Business Management.* Ely, England: IT Governance Publishing, 2013.

10 Hastie, Shane. "Standish Group 2015 Chaos Report — Q&A with Jennifer Lynch." InfoQ. October 4, 2015. Accessed July 28, 2017.
https://www.infoq.com/articles/standish-chaos-2015

11 The *12th Annual State of Agile Report.* VersionOne. April 9, 2108.
http://stateofagile.versionone.com/

12 Robson, Sharon and Shane Hastie. "Scaling Agile — It's All About the Context." SoftEd. September 4, 2013. Accessed January 9, 2018.
https://www.softed.com/news/scaling-agile-its-all-about-the-context

13. "Volatility, uncertainty, complexity and ambiguity." Wikipedia. Accessed January 9, 2018. https://en.wikipedia.org/wiki/Volatility,_uncertainty,_complexity_and_ambiguity

Part Seven

1. Leybourn, Evan. "#noprojects — Focus on Value, Not Projects." InfoQ. December 16, 2015. Accessed July 18, 2016. https://www.infoq.com/articles/noprojects2-focus-value

2. Wake, Bill. "INVEST in Good Stories, and SMART Tasks." XP123. August 17, 2003. Accessed November 5, 2016. http://xp123.com/articles/invest-in-good-stories-and-smart-tasks/

Part Eight

1. Gittleson, Kim. "Can a company live forever?" BBC News. January 19, 2012. Accessed June 3, 2017. http://www.bbc.com/news/business-16611040

2. "Employee Tenure Summary." Press release. US Bureau of Labor Statistics. September 22, 2016. Accessed October 1, 2016. http://www.bls.gov/news.release/tenure.nr0.htm

3. Senge, Peter M. *The Fifth Discipline: The Art and Practice of the Learning Organization.* New York: Doubleday, 1990.

4. Drucker, Peter F. "Managing for Business Effectiveness." *Harvard Business Review.* May, 1963. Accessed June 10, 2018. https://hbr.org/1963/05/managing-for-business-effectiveness

5. Goldratt, Eliyahu M. and Jeff Cox. *The Goal: A Process of Ongoing Improvement.* New York: North River Press, 2004.

6. O'Reilly, Barry. "How to Implement Hypothesis-Driven Development." ThoughtWorks. October 18, 2014. Accessed January 10, 2018. https://thoughtworks.com/insights/blog/how-implement-hypothesis-driven-development

7. O'Reilly. "Velocity 2011: Jon Jenkins, 'Velocity Culture'" YouTube video, 15:13. June 20, 2011. https://www.youtube.com/watch?v=dxk8b9rSKOo

8. Brown, Alanna et al. *2016 State of DevOps Report. Puppet + DORA.* 2016. Accessed June 10, 2018. https://puppet.com/resources/whitepaper/2016-state-of-devops-report

9. Bysouth, Stephanie. "Agile at Scale in an Enterprise Program." SlideShare. September 12, 2013. Accessed April 28, 2017. https://www.slideshare.net/stephaniebysouth/enterprise-program

10. Humble, Jez and David Farley. *Continuous Delivery: Reliable Software Releases through Build, Test, and Deployment Automation.* Boston, MA: Pearson Education, 2011.

11 "Real-time marketing," Wikipedia. Accessed January 10, 2018. https://en.wikipedia.org/wiki/Real-time_marketing

12 Leybourn, Evan. "#noprojects — Outcomes: The Value of Change." InfoQ. January 14, 2016. Accessed October 18, 2016. https://www.infoq.com/articles/noprojects3-value-change

Part Nine

1 Laloux, Frederic. *Reinventing Organizations*. Brussels: Nelson Parker, 2014.

2 Leybourn, Evan. *Directing the Agile Organisation: A Lean Approach to Business Management*. Ely, England: IT Governance Publishing, 2013.

3 Tuckman, Bruce W. "Developmental sequence in small groups." *Psychological Bulletin* 63, no. 6 (1965). doi:10.1037/h0022100.

4 Huckman, Robert S. and Bradley Staats. "The Hidden Benefits of Keeping Teams Intact." *Harvard Business Review*. December 2013. Accessed July 18, 2016. https://hbr.org/2013/12/the-hidden-benefits-of-keeping-teams-intact

5 Graham, Paul. "Maker's Schedule, Manager's Schedule." Paulgraham.com. July 2009. Accessed June 26, 2017. http://www.paulgraham.com/makersschedule.html

6 Deming, W. Edwards. *Out of the Crisis*. Cambridge, MA: Massachusetts Institute of Technology Press, 1982.

7 Schuman, Michael. "Zhang Ruimin's Haier Power." Haier. Accessed May 14, 2018. http://www.haier.net/en/about_haier/news/201404/t20140426_218091.shtml

8 Pomerantz, Dorothy, Samantha Shaddock, and Caroline Howard, eds. "The 100 Most Powerful Women." *Forbes*. August 27, 2008. Accessed May 14, 2018. http://www.forbes.com/lists/2008/11/biz_powerwomen08_Yang-Mian-Mian_UCN9.html

9 "Haier Tops Euromonitor's Major Appliances Global Brand Rankings for Seventh Consecutive Year." PR Newswire. January 20, 2016. Accessed May 14, 2018. http://www.prnewswire.com/news-releases/haier-tops-euromonitors-major-appliances-global-brand-rankings-for-seventh-consecutive-year-300206919.html

10 "Thinkers 50 IdeasLab China Established at Haier's Qingdao Headquarters!" Haier. Accessed May 14, 2018. http://www.haier.net/en/about_haier/news/201611/t20161116_327238.shtml

11 "Introduction to Haier's Overseas Market." Haier. Accessed May 14, 2018. http://www.haier.net/en/about_haier/haier_global/OverseasMarket/

12 Stengel, Jim. "Wisdom from the Oracle of Qingdao." *Forbes*. November 13, 2012. Accessed May 14, 2018. http://www.forbes.com/sites/jimstengel/2012/11/13/wisdom-from-the-oracle-of-qingdao/#73e09ba15e01

13. "Haier: Acquisition of GE Appliances Is Completed." Polymer Industry Media International. June 20, 2016. Accessed May 14, 2018. http://pimi.ir/haier-acquisition-ge-appliances-completed/.

14. Sprague, Jonathan. "Fortune: Haier Reaches Higher." Haier. September 16, 2002. Accessed May 14, 2018. http://www.haier.net/en/about_haier/news/201108/t20110817_52080.html

15. Day, Peter. "Smashing Way to Start a Global Business." BBC News. October 23, 2013. Accessed May 14, 2018. http://www.bbc.com/news/business-24622247

16. "Core Value of Haier." Haier. Accessed May 14, 2018. http://www.haier.net/en/about_haier/culture/

17. Liu, Cecily. "Taking customers to a Haier ground to serve them better." *China Daily*. August 16, 2013. Accessed May 14, 2018. http://usa.chinadaily.com.cn/business/2013-08/26/content_16920089.htm

18. Kleiner, Art. "China's Philosopher-CEO Zhang Ruimin." *Strategy+Business*. November 10, 2014. Accessed May 14, 2018. http://www.strategy-business.com/article/00296?gko=8155b

19. Mahajan, Neelima. "Haier's Zhang Ruimin: Challenge Yourself, Overcome Yourself," CKGSB Knowledge. September 30, 2015. Accessed May 14, 2018. http://knowledge.ckgsb.edu.cn/2015/10/07/china-business-strategy/haier-ceo-zhang-ruimin-challenge-yourself-overcome-yourself/

20. Fischer, Bill, Umberto Lago, and Fang Liu. "The Haier Road to Growth." *Strategy+Business*. April 27, 2015. Accessed May 14, 2018. http://www.strategy-business.com/article/00323?gko=c8c2a

Part Ten

1. Kniberg, Henrik. "Spotify engineering culture (part 2)." Spotify Labs. September 20, 2014. Accessed January 9, 2018. https://labs.spotify.com/2014/09/20/spotify-engineering-culture-part-2/

2. Seo, Ji-Won. *Excessive Overtime, Workers, and Productivity: Evidence and Implications for Better Work*. Geneva: International Labour Organization, 2011.

3. Veryanen, Marianna et al. "Overtime work and incident coronary heart disease: the Whitehall II prospective cohort study." *European Heart Journal 31, no. 14 (2010)*. doi: 10.1093/eurheartj/ehq124.

4. Proctor, Susan P. et al. "Effect of overtime work on cognitive function in automotive workers." *Scandinavian Journal of Work, Environment & Health 22, no. 2 (1996)*. doi: 10.5271/sjweh.120.

5. Macdonald, Wendy and Salaheddine Bendak. "Effects of workload and 8- versus 12-h workday duration on test battery performance." *International Journal of Industrial Ergonomics 26, no. 3 (2000)*. doi: 10.1016/S0169-8141(00)00015-9.

6 Hastie, Shane. "Lean-Agile Procurement for Outsourcing." InfoQ. April 16, 2018. Accessed May 13, 2018. https://www.infoq.com/news/2018/04/lean-agile-procurement

7 Bogsnes, Bjarte. *Implementing Beyond Budgeting: Unlocking the Performance Potential.* Hoboken, NJ: John Wiley & Sons, 2009.

Part Eleven

1 Leybourn, Evan. "Domains of Business Agility." The Agile Director. May 25, 2017. Accessed June 25, 2017. http://theagiledirector.com/article/2017/05/25/domains-of-business-agility-v2/

2 Denning, Steve. "More on Why Managers Hate Agile." *Forbes.* January 28, 2015. Accessed June 3, 2017. https://www.forbes.com/sites/stevedenning/2015/01/28/more-on-why-managers-hate-agile

3 Bogsnes, Bjarte. *Implementing Beyond Budgeting: Unlocking the Performance Potential.* Hoboken, NJ: John Wiley & Sons, 2009.

4 Denning, Steve. "What Is Business Agility?" Lecture. Business Agility 2017, New York. February 23, 2017. https://www.infoq.com/presentations/3-laws-business-agility

5 Drucker, Peter F. *Management: Tasks, Responsibilities, Practices.* New York: Harper & Row, 1974.

6 Leybourn, Evan. "The Mathematics of Agile Communication." The Agile Director. December 9, 2013. Accessed June 3, 2017. http://theagiledirector.com/article/2013/12/09/the-mathematics-of-agile-communication/

Printed in Great Britain
by Amazon